The Politics
of Repentance

The POLITICS of REPENTANCE

The Robert Treat Paine Lectures for 1951

by

ANDRÉ TROCMÉ

European Secretary of the
International Fellowship of Reconciliation

Translated by

John Clark

FELLOWSHIP PUBLICATIONS
21 Audubon Avenue
New York

Contents

INTRODUCTION

OUR RESPONSIBILITY HAS BEEN BEFORE US SINCE THE beginning of the world: Thou shalt love God; Thou shalt love thy neighbor. Everything springs from these two commandments.

But who is God? Who is my neighbor?—asks modern man. He doesn't know any longer. School, press and radio have initiated him into the growing complexity of a world that is ceaselessly being transformed by the technical progress of modern times. He is lost in his thinking. First, he says, I must find science's answer to my two questions; then I will act. But while he ponders, society crumbles. It is then that the men of action step in—capitalists, communists, fascists, soldiers and politicians—with the announcement: first we will act and establish order in the world; afterwards we will turn to the consideration of moral problems. But the action of these men, itself lacking order, leads the world into contradictions, and ultimately into war.

Thought and action are one. Separated they go round and round in circles and peter out. Together, as Jesus taught, they are the Life, or better, the Way and the Truth.

We shall be obliged in these pages to allude to certain political, social, philosophical or theological problems, but we shall try to remain within the reach of men unaccustomed to over-subtle reasoning. The central problem may be summed up in a sentence: what am I to tell my son and daughter about the meaning of life? how shall I teach them the significance of an earthly and eternal existence which sometimes I fear I have lost myself?

Our existence as human beings has several aspects or dimensions. Three are obvious. The first is our *physical* life, without which all the rest collapses. The second is our *mental* life. Our rational intelligence raises us above the animals and enables us to distinguish our "self" from the world around us. (Under the heading of intelligence, we include analytical or scientific thinking, as well as all attempts at synthesis based on rational, mystical or artistic intuition.)

The third dimension is *moral* and *social*. Man as a member of society is bound by moral obligation. Human societies are constantly developing religious myths and imposing respect for them on the individual.

We live in a world of three dimensions. Our spiritual life, no less than our physical, is three-dimensional. It is not within our power to escape from our own nature. The philosophers will tell us that we must stop our study here, that if there is something "beyond" the three dimensions already described, man is not capable of grasping it. At least, that is how they spoke before the war. But the experience of resistance and the dividing of the world into three ideological camps—liberal, Marxist and fascist— compel us to go beyond the limits of our world of three dimensions. Since 1939 it has become impossible to fit "the Good" into the traditional formulas taught by human societies, or even by the churches. An uneasiness and a growing tension are apparent.

The moral person feels himself compelled to oppose society and, often, the church. This opposition, even more than his submission to established laws, underlines the moral character of man. Just as in the physical order Einstein has demonstrated to us the existence of a fourth dimension, which we cannot perceive but only calculate, so the essence of our own being is under the shadow of a fourth dimension which cannot be rationalized nor described, but only recognized and believed—the Christian dimension. (We do not say "divine" dimension because too many things have been classed under the heading "God," but "Christian" dimension because it has been revealed to us by Jesus.) We shall decorate it with weak, well-worn phrases: "sacrifice of the Cross," "redeeming love," "atoning death" and so on. We shall attempt to express the impossible and we shall always fail. Geometry permits us to construct an object with three dimensions, but not with four. In the same way, a geometry of the Christian faith is an impossibility. The "cur deus homo?" will always remain unanswered.

The fourth dimension is the key to all the others. From the moment I receive light from above, in fear, adoration and fervent gratitude I am able to manipulate the mysterious lock of the moral world. The moral dimension, clarified, opens up the mystery of the intelligence. My regenerated intelligence unravels the tangle of my physical existence. Thus the world is built on the inexplicable. (Inexplicable does not mean unreal.) It is a matter of historical fact, the fact of the birth of a child destined for the Cross, a fact neither more nor less inexplicable than any other birth, but just as real in the three dimensions we have described—*plus the fourth,* which was revealed at that moment.

The Politics
of Repentance

Part One

THE PHYSICAL AND RATIONAL DIMENSIONS

Chapter 1

The Highest Good

OUR PERSONAL BODILY LIFE IS OUR ONLY REAL POSSES-
sion. All other riches depend upon it. The dead have
nothing. Religious faith assures us that they live on or are
born again in one way or another, but it gives us no
proof.

On the other hand, I do have proof of the existence of
the world, of its beauty and grandeur, its variety, its stars,
and the beings that inhabit it. My five senses are my life.
I see, I touch, I hear, I smell, I taste, and so come to
know that other people, other things exist. If I retire
within myself, I am not always very sure of my own
existence. But ever since I was a child, others have said
that they see me, touch me, hear me, smell me, taste me;
so I conclude that I too exist, and I take the game of
existence seriously. But if I have an accident and lose
consciousness, I am no longer aware of anything. A piece
of the world of the senses has crumbled and disappeared
with the consciousness of one human being. If all men
and women, one after the other, were to become uncon-

3

scious without dying, there would no longer be anyone to see the world, no people to touch, hear, smell, taste each other in the human manner. Then the world would be perceived as cows, ants or whales perceive it; but everything leads us to suppose that their world is very different from ours.

So, our individual life is something essential. It is the lens without which no image of the world can appear on any screen. Its continued existence is a condition of the existence of the world itself. Humanity is not a collective person whose five senses are endowed with the power of perception. Everything happens at the level of the individual human being. Mankind in its history, its literature, its music, its religion, its civilization, is conscious only in the soul of each man taken individually. Indeed we are permitted to hope that there is a supreme being who sees, touches, hears, tastes and smells our earth, and that he is more completely aware of it than we are, under forms of which we know nothing. We may think that in his eyes there is meaning in human history. We may hold that if the world were destroyed, he would remain. Personally I believe this. But at the beginning of this book we will place ourselves on ground common with all men and consider first the undeniable fact on which we can agree at the outset: I am living, you are living, we exist. Each one of us, on a certain day, entered the world from his mother's womb. This minute event conditions all the rest, and we must make it the first object of our interest.

I am as sure of dying one day as I am sure of having been born. Thoughts of my end and fear of the suffering that will precede my death weave in the depths of my being a gray fabric which I strive to render as colorless as possible so as not to fall into despondency. But man carries within himself a deep sense of the value of existence. He devotes all his efforts to maintaining and improving it. Food, clothing, shelter, comfort (and the work we do to provide ourselves with them), social organization, the state, commerce, industry, transportation, medicine and science—all have as their object the protection and perpetuation of our existence as individuals. That it should be so is good and valid, we have no doubt. On the other hand, death and the sickness that leads to it are bad, enemies of our existence. If a man to whom I have done nothing kills me, he is a criminal. If he kills deliberately thousands of individuals like myself, he commits the crime of crimes in annihilating a portion of the world's consciousness. He is the anti-man, the anti-existence, the anti-creator.

But let us go a step further. My life is at the center of things, since it conditions the existence of everything else. But I should fall victim to a senseless and ridiculous pride if I failed to recognize at the same time the existence of other men. When I think of others, it is not a question of statistics. I know there are more than two thousand million people on the earth, but my mind is not capable of grasping this figure. Rather, as Jesus said, the other man is this other self, quite as real as my own, quite as central, this self which I meet in the street, on a battlefield, or in my home. The essence of all the higher religions is summed up in two commandments. The first is *Thou shalt love God,* which means you are to love him who is. You exist, therefore, and you resemble him, for no one can love what is unlike himself. This comes to the same thing as saying that God loves you, or again, that the secret of the universe is that your life has an absolute value. And this is the second commandment: *Thou shalt love thy neighbor as thyself.* That is to say, your neighbor is as real as you are and deserves quite as much consideration. To destroy or to harm his life, that is, his senses, is an offense against the whole creation no less criminal than the destruction of your own life.

On these two points common sense agrees with religion. Some people are quick to sympathize with their neighbors' misfortunes. They are often capable of sharing them. It is not the same, alas, with all people. Some have lost the way that leads to the other man; regarding themselves as members of a superior race, class, nation, religion or party, they cease to have a concrete view of him; they classify him, put him in a category, call him Negro, Chinese, barbarian, communist, or capitalist. And then they assume the right to despise him and the duty of killing him.

Yet there is good in modern civilization: it facilitates human contacts, multiplies exchanges of men and ideas to such an extent that class and race prejudices are constantly disappearing. It has become necessary for governments that wish to utilize the force of public opinion for national defense to safeguard it by erecting huge artificial barriers of censorship and propaganda. Otherwise the peoples are apt to reconcile themselves with one another. Anyone who has traveled from one country to another knows that simple people everywhere, hearing for the first time about conscientious objectors, exclaim: "They refuse to kill? How right they are; if we all did the same, there would be no more war! Ah, if only we were united!" This

naïve judgment implies a condemnation, which is justified, of the ever more artificial systems which lead men to
collective massacres. We will consider later whether the
common sense of the people is practical. But let us rejoice
here and now that common sense still exists. War has become a source of absurdity. It is impossible today to believe in the validity of our own existence if we deny the
validity of our neighbor's. By perpetuating outdated con-
ceptions we are preparing a pitiful generation of young
skeptics who, knowing themselves to be dedicated to the
hangman's job, despise to the highest degree their own
existence. "Kill, be killed; what does it matter?" we hear
them say. "My life has no value, no more than any other
lives. The day I was born in spite of myself I was deceived
by a blind fate."

Only a few years ago we could still kill with conviction.
We believed sincerely that men were divided into good
and bad, and that the bad were on the other side of a
frontier. *They* were the essential obstacle to the triumph
of good on earth. Therefore *they* must be destroyed. Today such beliefs are no longer admitted. They are perpetuated by Machiavellian governments, themselves un-
believing, but driven on by the political necessity which
governs their decisions. But man is believing less and less
in his own goodness and the radical wickedness of others.
He kills without conviction, like the tool of an aimless
fate. The state invokes its laws, the rules of the community. Most of us still obey them because we are afraid
of being alone against the mass, but few believe any
longer in the sovereign wisdom of these laws. To find men
who are convinced, men whose purity is absolute and joy-
ful, you must often go to the prisons. There you will meet

a few transparent beings who can tell you quite simply:
"I believe in God who is love; I believe that God loves me
and that he loves my neighbor, even if my neighbor is my
enemy, even if he is the enemy of God himself." Against
the crystal-clearness of such an attitude, traditional laws
are powerless. Courts condemn, throw into prison, and,
under totalitarian rule, deport, execute and behead. It
makes no difference: there are always conscientious objectors, and there will always be more and more of them,
because any other attitude is absurd. Their behavior
alarms the theologians, who ally themselves surprisingly
with atheist philosophy. Theories are hastily hammered
out to isolate the objectors, just as a forest fire is isolated
to restrict the damage. "It's a matter of individual vocation," they say. "Nonviolence has no social significance.
It is an independent gesture of despair, with the sole merit
of reminding men that their final end is not earthly."

The wars and tyrannies of modern times are sufficient
in themselves to demonstrate their own absurdity. After
each wave of collective insanity, when the nightmare is
over, it becomes clear that the conscientious objector was
right. The thousands of Jehovah's Witnesses who resisted
Hitler and perished in the concentration camps did more
for Germany than the millions of Nazi soldiers who,
obedient to the state, set out to conquer Europe. The conscientious objectors in America who today will not allow
themselves to be mobilized are doing more to check the
fall of democratic civilization in imperialistic pride than
the millions of civilizers in uniform who hope to save freedom with the atomic bomb.

If the Marxist revolution undertakes to dominate the
world by terror, it will destroy itself, though not before

murdering millions of innocent people. But the disciples of Tolstoy and of all the genuine representatives of the soul of the Russian people, humble victims of persecution today, are even now preparing a future for their country.

Chapter 2

Sacrifice

Besides the instinct that impels us to respect our own lives and our neighbors', there is another, no less certain: the instinct of self-sacrifice. Voluntary in the hero and the saint, conscious in the mother, vaguely present in the masses, the instinct of self-sacrifice leads humanity as surely as the instinct of self-preservation. It exists already in the animal world—and with what force! Jesus expressed the need in a revealing sentence: "He who will save his life shall lose it." There is, then, a value higher than physical life, and for this it is right to die. Sometimes it is the social group—family, tribe, nation, party, humanity—which claims our utter devotion; and the man who shirks his duty knows he is a coward. Sometimes it is religion that tears us from our egoism and exacts from us the supreme sacrifice; and the man who avoids it knows he is unfaithful.

These principles, for which we are asked to sacrifice every possession, are called ideals. Every group professes an ideal. I know that the communists will deny having one, but that makes no difference to the fact. The moment you contrast "the-world-as-it-ought-to-be" with "the-world-as-it-is" you become an idealist. This does not mean that a moral sense must be attached to the word "ought." If I say that the subsequent social transformation must "necessarily" take place, I am already an idealist, because to the world-as-it-is-today I oppose the world-as-it-will-necessarily-be-tomorrow. Moreover, I affirm my idealism far more by my conduct and my ability to renounce my individual existence for the sake of a future common good, than by the vocabulary, more or less spiritual or materialist, I may care to use. Every man who is able to give his life in the service of a common cause asserts, even without knowing it, that there are values superior to that of individual existence.

If today we possessed a formula whereby a man in giving himself could be sure of saving many others, the moral tension in which we live would relax instantly. Look at the serene calm of those whose vocation it is to devote themselves wholly to saving the lives of their neighbors: Sisters of Mercy, lifeboatmen, stretcher-bearers, firemen, missionaries, doctors or nurses working in constant danger of infection. The courageous soldier because he may be killed at any moment is surrounded with the same halo of glory. By giving his life he hopes to save the lives of others. It is the secret link between thirst for sacrifice and concern for the salvation of others that still calls so many noble souls to a military career. Indeed, not many years ago the soldier at the front could still hope that his body was protecting the wife and children he had left behind. This is where our modern tragedy begins. The European soldier of 1939 often returned, himself safe and sound, only to find his home destroyed, his loved ones, for whose protection his sacrifice was no longer sufficient, dead. This is the point to which the progress of military technique has brought us. No one can be held responsible for this cheating of heroism, and yet it is a terrible swindle to which the idealist thirsting for devotion falls victim today. What is absurd, however, is that, believing in good faith that he is saving the group to which he belongs, he finds himself transformed into an instrument of annihilation. He inflicts on the "enemy" group terrible human losses, without the satisfaction even of checking the evildoer or of saving his own group from destruction. Modern war decides nothing, leaving victors and vanquished, heroes and cowards, innocent and guilty in the same ruin. That is why it can no longer be justified.

And yet a final possibility of justifying military sacrifice would be open to us if we could show either that (a) the existence of higher civilizations, that is, of those which offer the best protection for human life, is threatened by lower civilizations, or that (b) civilizations regarded as "superior" prevail over the inferior in war.

Then, the legitimate defense of a higher culture attacked by an enemy from a lower stage of civilization would be justified.

If there are in fact "superior" and "inferior" civilizations, we must decide in what respect they protect human life more or less effectively. Such a judgment is subjective in character. What form of society is most favorable to human life? A society that affords equality of political rights, that is, maximum liberty of thought and action? Or is it the society that guarantees equality of economic rights, that is, maximum protection against exploitation?

Depending on my personal tendencies, and often according to the social class or nation to which I belong, I judge that such and such a form of social organization is superior. Without knowing it, I make a value judgment. Each society, each social class, each nation judges subjectively that *it* is the best, without any possible guarantee of the objective validity of such a judgment. Hence wars and the relentlessness of wars.

But perhaps war, as the instrument of a providential fate, is a brutal but effective means of selecting the "best" civilizations? Are we to believe in this historical Darwinism whereby progress would be realized by a survival of the fittest? Let us observe at once that the knowledge we have today of the workings of evolution goes beyond Darwin's over-simplified analysis. Causes other than their fitness to survive have led to the birth, rise and fall of species. And it is the same with civilizations, as the English historian Toynbee has shown. They have perished or survived for internal reasons which are not all bound up with military victories or defeats. Jerusalem and Athens, although conquered, survived. Babylon and Rome, conquering, perished. The problem of the triumph of ideological values is much more complex than at first appears. If, however, the triumph or destruction of a civilization is determined by war, it would be well to return to the polytheism of the ancient world, in which the dubious outcome of the wars waged unceasingly by the gods in heaven made or marred the fortunes of the nations. Each generation would be destined for endless bleeding on the hostile altars of insatiable deities. Unless, O blasphemy, wars serve the purposes of the One God in the accomplishing of his mysterious and man-devouring

will. Such is the strange metaphysic to which we are led
by our desire to reconcile modern war with the nobleness
of voluntary sacrifice on the one hand and the service
of eternal "values" on the other. Let us be simpler then,
more childlike, and ask ourselves if human history has not
reached the point where war and the thirst for sacrifice
must be separated.

"Principles," let us state clearly, no longer have anything to do with wars. Of all the deceptions of history,
war is the most monstrous. It enrolls the noblest of men in
the service of a tragic illusion. It is in fact no more than a
survival of primitive barbarism linked with the symptoms
of a premature decline in civilization, in which belief in
blood sacrifice, the primitive pride of the clan, the savage
instinct of domination and destruction, the inconceivable
stupidity of fear-stricken masses, the monstrous imbecility
or colossal vanity of their leaders are joined to the conscientious—I would say "religious"—diligence with
which the virtues of soldiers and technicians are applied
to the perfecting of methods of destruction. The combination of these virtues, superstitions and vices results at
regular intervals in the refined organization of massacres
which become ever more spectacular and useless. In fact,
what modern war destroys is not the savage but the
civilized. It no longer conquers deserts, it ravages universities; it no longer brings the benefits of science to backward peoples, it plants the tents of barbarians in the ruins
of Athens. There are no more just wars, no more defensive wars; there are only wars of annihilation. Everything
leads us to believe that it will be worse tomorrow than it
is today. What becomes, then, of the two values we have
considered fundamental: "human life" and "society-as-

it-ought-to-be" as opposed to society-as-it-is? Not much. Human life is destroyed without scruple. As for "society-as-it-ought-to-be," the possibility of realizing it will disappear in the convulsions now being prepared. When the world is given up to famine, disorder and useless vengeance, the principle of "every man for himself" will prevail. Mankind will lose sight of today's great dreams; parliamentary democracy will wither; the socialism yet to be born will appear as a distorted Marxism, maintaining its hold over the minds of men by terror and the imposition of a pseudoscientific mythology; the idea of a world government will vanish.

Established religions, the Christian church at their head, seem to have abandoned already the two sacred causes which were their particular concerns in past centuries: they no longer defend human life; they no longer provide places of refuge against barbarism; they no longer found "hospitals" to shelter the fleeing multitudes of our time. No longer, in this twentieth century, do they free the slaves; they are no longer capable even of inspiring, in the name of a better world, the spirit of sacrifice in their members. Men die today for a country, or a political party, on a battlefield, in an airplane, a tank, a concentration camp, a prison cell, under torture, but only rarely for God, at the stake or on the gallows, lonely martyrs mocked by the crowd, with the smile of faith on their lips greeting from afar the final triumph of love.

Individual life, we said earlier, is the only certain value in this world. We added that an individual should sacrifice his own life if he is sure that by doing so he can save a greater number of his fellows. We observed, finally, that no one can be sure today of saving his fellows by means of war. There remains then only one way open: the way of conscientious objection; only so can I be sure of not destroying the very essence of existence—as a man who gives his life to save others and at the same time refuses to kill others, friends or enemies. But an argument is often raised: Is not your abstention going to favor the enterprises of exploiters and men of violence? In withdrawing from the human drama are you not trying to wash your hands of it, are you not becoming the hypocritical accomplice in the crimes that are committed? Here is not yet the place to reply to this objection. Remaining on practical ground, we will content ourselves now with asking: Does there exist a method of defending and saving the human person which does not involve the extermination of human beings? If there is no such method, then in the name of a holy realism, and because we believe in the central importance of man's individual existence, we will reject conscientious objection. But if it is proved, historically, that objectors save human life, then we must back them. It is better to concentrate our energies on perfecting constructive methods for man's salvation than to exhaust ourselves killing him in the vain hope of saving him.

Chapter 3

Salvation

HISTORY PROVIDES NUMEROUS EXAMPLES OF SAINTS who have saved individuals and communities by the power of the spirit. We are no longer capable of discerning that power. How can a country like France, whose capital was saved from the Normans by the prayer of St. Genevieve, doubt the strength of those who put their trust in the sovereign power of good? Can St. Genevieve be accused of standing hypocritically aside at the moment when Paris was threatened? Father Lorson in his book *Can a Christian Be a Conscientious Objector?* quotes the examples of St. Maximilian, St. Victrice, bishop of Rouen at the end of the 4th century, St. Martin of Tours, the Curé of Ars. Voltaire, the skeptic, was still capable of penetrating the history of his own time when he praised the Quaker experiment in Pennsylvania. Alone among the American colonists, the Quakers lived in peace with the Indians because they practiced Christian nonviolence. In the twelve other colonies of the new continent, it was considered that the only way to save the lives of the white people was to kill the redskins. The redskin race was al-most obliterated. How many innocent whites perished in this tragedy? And more, how far did the violence of the 17th and 18th centuries sow the seeds of today's Ameri-can nationalism? Where is man's salvation? Have not England in granting India her liberty, or Holland in giving up Indonesia, done more for the salvation of the Europeans than France in her war with Indo-China?

The 19th century, the sad 19th century, paved the way to the tragic dead-end of the 20th. The bloody "civiliz-ing" conquests among colonial peoples have sown the seeds of African and Asiatic vengeance, which will prob-ably fill the second half of the 20th century with blood-shed. The white race thought it could conquer the world. Very likely it has prepared its own downfall. Already today it is on the defensive, and defending itself with difficulty. Yet nonviolence was not absent from the 19th century. The history of Christian missions, of which the public at large is totally ignorant, provides a marvelous catalogue of martyrs. The life of the great contemporary Frenchman, Albert Schweitzer, brings it up to date. Hun-dreds of believers in nonviolence, emulating David Liv-ingstone, set out to bring the spirit of Christ to unknown lands. They did not save human lives, you will say, not even their own. How wrong you are! Long before the conquering armies arrived to occupy the country, the missionaries were opening hospitals, teaching hygiene, caring for lepers. It is not true, as is often claimed, that colonial conquests have opened the way to Christian mis-sions. Rather they have marked the beginning of their decay. Missions becoming prosperous have been led to rely more on material power and military protection than on prayer. But the good had already been done. The peoples of Asia and Africa were awakening. At the moment when the torch was slipping from the hands of the whites, Gandhi, inspired by Jesus without being converted to a failing Christianity, undertook the task of liberating his people and driving the foreigners from control of his country without the use of violence. His wonderful adventure has been related elsewhere. We will say simply that Gandhi was not one who stood aside: twenty-five years of campaigning against an unjust occupation, the painstaking organization of national strikes and campaigns of non-cooperation against the English, together with his perfect objectivity and his power of prayer which enabled him to temper mass movements when they threatened to become violent—all this has freed India without bloodshed. Millions of lives have been saved. The desired result has been obtained. And what is more, India has not since been carried away by nationalistic pride, hatred and moral disorder as she would have been after a war of liberation.

As soon as the example of India is quoted, objections are offered. Gandhi had to deal with the English, an orderly people, accustomed to a certain self-control, and deeply enough religious to recognize the quality of their adversary. Agreed; and what does that prove if not that a religious attitude and respect for one's opponent can profoundly modify the terms of a political problem? If Gandhi had had to deal with the Germans or the Russians, say those who question the value of his example, he would have been shot at dawn without trial. But Pastor Niemöller was not shot by Hitler, and his resistance to Nazism at least saved the honor of the Christian church in Germany. The tyrants of all ages, like Herod with John the Baptist, have listened secretly to the voices of prophets. Even if, in the future, enterprises of the Gandhi type were to be destined to political failure, even if the principle of nonviolence were never to appear at the head of a world constitution, it would remain nonetheless true that the history of the world is not solely political. Politics is probably the common factor which day by day captures the anxious attention of the greatest percentage of human beings. Yet schools and universities, hospitals and laboratories, museums and academies, churches and theaters, agriculture and industry, commerce and transportation absorb a much greater part of human thought and activity. In none of these fields is the destruction of human life considered indispensable.

On the contrary, the hypnotizing influence of the political hysteria and emotions of the day is excluded from them. Churchmen and philanthropists have other things to do than to adapt their ways of thinking to the laws of today's rulers. But here again there is an objection. Gandhi was a leader of the Indian people, whose religion is fundamentally nonviolent, who are accustomed to being passive, and whose nature is simple and trusting. Western peoples, realistic and materialistic in outlook, are too far removed from such a mode of thought and action to be able to make use of it. This objection made Gandhi smile when he came to Geneva before the war: "If our spiritual and intellectual resources were as great as yours in Europe," he said, "what should we not have already accomplished in India!" He was right. Nowhere in the world does there exist an instrument of thought, education and discipline comparable to the Christian church.

Nowhere is faith so reflective and so profound. Christian
doctrine is fundamentally nonviolent, as is Hindu doctrine. If the peoples of the West have become realists and
materialists, it is because their prosperity has turned them
from their religion. In reality they are as open to faith
and to collective action as the peoples of the East. The
Western masses, as in the Middle Ages, are constantly
roused by prospects of reform, followed, alas, by disillusionment in the absence of leaders to give spiritual direction. The extraordinary success which the campaign for
world citizenship met at its beginning, the naïvely en-
thusiastic welcome given to the Stockholm appeal, are
proof. It is not the people who lack faith, but their
leaders. Political leaders, corrupted by a diplomatic and
military Machiavellism inherited from our imperialistic
past, are ironical about the advocates of absolute principles who believe they can change the world. Religious
leaders, led astray by the prosperity of the church, have
ceased to believe in good. They describe it, but no longer
think it can be attained. Their catechism tells man:
"Sinner thou art, sinner thou wilt remain. Society causes
thee to sin, religion gives thee absolution. Choose, therefore, the lesser evil. Above all, avoid yielding to the pride
of believing thyself called to practice the Gospel."

Part Two

THE "MORAL-RELIGIOUS" DIMENSION

Chapter 4

Society-as-it-ought-to-be vs. Society-as-it-is

F ROM EARLIEST TIMES MEN HAVE ORGANIZED THEM-
selves into societies. None of us can live alone. Whenever
a pure and original soul seeks to base his life on rules laid
down by his conscience or derived from a religious absolute, he clashes severely with society. Family, school, fac-
tory, commercial customs, army, state and even established religion, all rebuke him. If you want to live in
absolute purity, leave the civilized world and find a desert
island where you can be a law unto yourself. And even
there you will depend on others to supply you with the
things you cannot do without. You cannot cut yourself
off from your fellows. Therefore you must accept society's
rules. Now the social order was not made in a day. It is
the fruit of your ancestors' struggles and conquests.
France's, America's, continued existence depends on the
will of its citizens. By refusing to obey its laws, even in
the name of what you believe to be a higher ideal, you
undermine the permanence, the existence of your coun-

try. If everybody did as you are doing, there would soon
be nothing but hopeless anarchy on the earth, when the
only "law" would be the "conscience," or rather, the
whims and fancies, of each and every one. If you find
society imperfect, endeavor to change it by improving its
laws.

This reasoning is impressive. How many young men,
filled with zeal for the absolute, have been overcome by
it. They accept the necessary compromises, bury their
scruples, check their rebellious impulses. They return to
the ranks of the "good citizens," those who serve their
country faithfully in its established form. Yet France, for
example, in spite of heroic service during the colonial conquests, in three wars against Germany, and during the
Resistance, is on the point of going under. Why? Because
no forms of society are permanent in the world. A country that claims the right to govern consciences must
prove that it represents an optimum social order which
cannot be surpassed. Now in Europe today nation-states
are out of date. The Second World War has shown that
the national framework is too narrow. A country that
shuts itself up, as Spain has, dies of suffocation. France
fought against Germany in 1940. Beaten, she collaborated and adopted laws originating in Berlin. Liberated,
she returned to her traditional institutions. But the numerous civil servants and officers who, from motives of
loyalty, carried out the policies of Marshal Petain
learned in 1944 that they were traitors. These experiences
have matured the political judgment of the French. A
blind loyalty to the state is not enough. Not only the
peoples occupied by Germany, but the Germans themselves have experienced a similar crisis. They have learned

with their victims to distinguish between what the state dictates as expressing the true and the good, and the real truth, the real good, which are supranational in character. Today a similar problem is facing the satellites of Russia and the colonial peoples, as well as the troops who have intervened in Korea and Indo-China. In the final analysis, the citizen cannot avoid deciding for himself what is the true good for his country. It is the problem of society-as-it-ought-to-be against society-as-it-is. At the world level today we are bound to recognize the need for a world government. The moment we do so, we must choose between UN and the Soviet proposals for the reorganization of the world. We cannot remain neutral nor fail to recognize that our little country, France, must be fitted into a larger framework: Atlantic Union, United Europe, Popular Democracy.

There is something heartening in this dynamic aspect of the contemporary world. Never since the beginning of time has strict conservatism had less significance: everywhere new combinations are being formed. Never have the rules of blind obedience to the national community been less valid. We are told that the loyalty demanded of the young soldier for the defense of parliamentary France today will benefit the united Europe still to be born. Yes, indeed! But this united Europe will tomorrow become a part of either the Western hemisphere, the American, or the Eastern hemisphere, the Russian. The unreflecting masses will follow their masters and when the time comes, accept the truth of the propaganda dictated to them. But we who are less credulous must choose now, at our own risk, which cause is to be served: West or East, hegemony of the Western peoples or of the Slavs. The de-

cision lies with the individual. But the individual can be
mistaken.

It is here that the real political and social problem of
our time appears. History is committed. No one creates
it in accordance with his own wishes. We are born into it.
A politician, a government never has to deal with an isolated situation. To say: Why don't Mr. Eisenhower and
Mr. Malenkov act according to the standards of the Sermon on the Mount: "Love your enemies, resist not evil";
why don't they disarm their countries and shake hands?
is to be very naïve. The President of the United States,
carried to power by public elections, is master neither of
the opinions nor of the interests of his people, nor of the
attitude and outlook of the adversary with whom he has
to deal. Is Malenkov much more free? Can any head of
state take the same risks on behalf of his people as he
would perhaps be free to take for himself as a private
individual? Even if he wanted to, public opinion would
not allow him. Thus, the President of the United States,
responsible in spite of himself for a rudimentary world
order which must be preserved, aims at running a minimum of risks for the United Nations. Recent history has
taught him that the League of Nations collapsed because
it did not, at the required moment, impose sanctions on
Mussolini as aggressor in Abyssinia; unwilling to repeat
this crime of abstention against a budding world organization, the President, backed by a majority of the member
nations of the UN, imposed sanctions on North Korea
for its aggression against South Korea. Will the Korean
war save the UN from premature ruin? The Americans
hope it will. It was better, they say, to intervene in a
conflict of minor importance for the purpose of giving a

lesson than to allow future aggressors to imagine that they can attack the weak with impunity. Our show of force will prevent a third world war. The young American conscripts have accepted the Korean war because they believe that their sacrifice is contributing to the organization of the "world-as-it-ought-to-be" according to the Western formula. "Our hands are not clean," they say, "but we are sacrificing our purity and our lives for the sake of a better world in which the word 'freedom' will not be meaningless." The majority of Christians in America consider, unenthusiastically, that it would be a crime against Western civilization, as trustee of dearly won liberties, not to support their government in its efforts to maintain order in the world. Western rearmament, they say, has no other object than to make the Russians understand that aggression doesn't pay. Faced with two evils, it is a religious duty to choose the lesser. Rearmament is certainly risky, a heavy responsibility, but it is better to rearm than to let the communists, and the peoples who are still wavering, think that democracy is weak. In Rome, Paris and London is not the reasoning the same? It is necessary to reassure the unstable masses as to the stability of the regimes that guarantee the church religious liberties, and that maintain the existing order in the French Union or the English Commonwealth.

Alas, it is not very difficult to put all these arguments into Russian. Once it is a question of the "world-as-it-ought-to-be" as opposed to the "world-as-it-is" there is no limit to the latitude of thought allowed. The Western nations think that the world can be reorganized on the model of a federal republic of the American type. Such an idea, the Marxists will say, is a sign of bourgeois and reactionary minds, ignorant of the deeper laws of the economic world, and fanatically attached to their privileges. Marx has shown that parliamentary liberalism guarantees to the exploited classes none of their fundamental freedoms. The UN is only a façade behind which are concealed the interests of the capitalist classes who want to keep the rest of the world under their domination. American intervention in Korea, if we had allowed it to develop, would have destroyed the confidence of the Asiatic peoples in the young popular democracy of China. It was a matter of life and death for the democracy and, therefore, for the future of the revolution. The moment the integrity of the Chinese frontiers was threatened, the spontaneous reaction of the communist volunteers became inevitable. To give proof of weakness was to ruin the future of a world which should, and can, reorganize itself only on a basis of social justice, that is, by the abolition of private capitalism. The revolution will advance slowly; it will progress only where capitalism itself demonstrates its own absurdity. We await patiently the destructive effects of its lack of internal equilibrium, but meanwhile our efforts cannot be relaxed; each one of us must be alert at his post for the defense of a regime of justice which alone can insure the peace of the world. For the time being, peace can only be defended by armed force, so long as the intentions of the capitalist world tend so plainly toward aggression and oppression. Do not events in Korea, Indo-China, Malaya, Persia, Egypt, Madagascar, South Africa, Tunisia and Morocco demonstrate the determination of the occupying powers to maintain their privileges at all costs?

Arguments like these can be used successively in support of all political positions. Each one contains a certain truth. The choice between the truths rests finally with the individual.

Chapter 5

What Is Truth?

WHEN PILATE ASKED JESUS, "WHAT IS TRUTH?",
Jesus did not reply. He had already given his answer in
affirming three things: first, truth is "not of this world";
secondly, he came to bear witness to the truth; thirdly,
whoever "has the truth" listens to his voice. For him,
truth is identical with God, but God is not a reality that
can be grasped by the intellect, nor yet a doctrine to
which we can assent, but a light or a divine word received
when we "act on the truth." Thus, truth is a *way* taken
by man on which, as he walks, he can verify the genuine-
ness of the spirit leading him. So as not to leave his disciples groping, Jesus declared to them, moreover, that he
himself was the way to the truth. An extraordinary asser-
tion, the value of which can be tested only by accepting
Jesus as the way that leads to God.

If we reject the teaching of Jesus concerning the nature
of truth, and therefore at the same time the teaching of
all the great religious masters, we shall conclude that
there is no suprahuman truth but only a more or less ade-

WHAT IS TRUTH? 33

quate human knowledge of the phenomena of our universe. We shall accept the notion that truths are products of human societies, and we shall act accordingly.

If, on the other hand, we accept the teaching of Jesus, we shall affirm the suprahuman character of truth, admit that it is eternal and that it judges societies, and act accordingly.

First hypothesis: truth is not suprahuman. For more than a century, sociologists have been teaching that religious truths are only the sublimated expression of society at a certain stage of economic and social development. Each society has its own gods and its own morality, which it imposes on its members in the form of religious myths. As history progresses, man invents new gods, provisional dogmas, in a succession that may be described as expressing the "progress" of morals.

If we subscribe to this brilliant theory, backed by thousands of scientific observations, we are led to concern ourselves very seriously with the social groups now in existence, for it is they that form the very web of history. We shall study, with or without Karl Marx, the natural laws which govern the rise and fall of societies.

We shall endeavor to deduce from them the meaning of history, that is to say, the direction in which it is moving. As social physicians, we shall study the functioning of societies and prescribe preventive medicines to protect them from sickness, or remedies to cure them. We shall be led to share the view of Marx and all materialists that the health of societies depends upon the equilibrium of the economic substructure. Nevertheless, as good historic materialists, we shall not accept the working out of the economic laws as fatally inevitable, but having realized how they operate, we shall, by means of large-scale planning, safeguard the economic prosperity of the social organism of which we are members (almost believers). Public education will be controlled in the same way. It will form minds for the service of the economic regime in which my nation, my race, my class find their expression. In this way, the state will guarantee itself good servants (we could say good priests, who maintain the worship of the truth peculiar to it).

It will be necessary also to look to the defense of the social group threatened from without by other societies expressing themselves in other truths, foreign and hostile to its own. This defense will be assured, if need be, by force of arms. The real creator of its own truth is the group itself. In fact, the group is the truth. As such, it has not the right to run the risk of being eliminated. If it disappears, its message to the world disappears. Hitler showed admirable understanding of the teaching of the sociological school when he declared: The German nation is the bearer of a truth which it has not the right to allow to deteriorate. The Jewish race is the bearer of another truth, foreign to the German truth and which challenges it. Our first duty toward our race is to purify it of the foreign presence. Let the Jews quit our soil and return to Palestine, or we will exterminate them. Truth is what serves the German race.

Before Hitler, Lenin had developed a similar theory. The proletarian class sees its day of triumph approaching, for its triumph is written in the inexorable development of economic conditions. Nevertheless, capitalism, clinging to the shreds of its outworn privileges, will do everything in its power to hinder the advent of the proletariat. It will not hesitate to make war; it will endeavor to corrupt the revolutionary society from within. To safeguard the purity of the revolution, we shall be obliged to adopt methods of unprecedented severity. But what matter? The truth is what serves the proletariat.

Is the liberal West so far removed from these ideas? Does not the worship of free enterprise, with the economic foundation it postulates for all other freedoms, gather many admirers in its temple? Are not Western societies dangerously tempted by fascism? Creators of their own truth, are they not apt to expel from their midst doctrines which are dangerous and impure? Claiming to offer themselves in the service of a supreme truth, are they not in fact putting their own salvation at the center of everything and chaining captive to the chariot of the defense of the free world a truth mutilated and enslaved? that truth is what insures the survival of parliamentary democracy and economic liberalism.

But we don't stop there. It is not impossible, after all, that men actually are forsaken and that they themselves do help to create their own truths. Perhaps every god does depend upon the success of an economic regime, a social class, or a race. Then the moral future of the world would be determined on the battlefield. If a third world war broke out between a West with a Christian majority and an East with a materialist majority, it is possible that the military defeat of the West might entail the ruin of Christianity. Our grandchildren would stop going to catechism, and would be instructed in the worship of the proletariat. If such were in fact the case, then we should have to defend the god we favor, take up arms on his behalf before it was too late to save him. The slightest failure on our part would be a crime against the truth. All our undertakings ought to be dominated, then, by the most concrete realism. The scruples causing us to hesitate before a war of aggression would have to be cast aside. The society to which I belong would be sole judge of good and evil, that is, of what does or does not contribute to its survival. A well-planned atomic offensive, a premeditated act of aggression launched at the right moment, that is to say, when the opponent is weak and I can hope to beat him with a minimum of bloodshed, a well-coordinated attack, a Blitzkrieg utilizing all the resources of total war could, I say, be the most highly moral act I could commit, for it would contribute toward strengthening the position of my nation in the world and thus toward developing the success of the truth it embodies.

But let us go yet a step further. Let us speak in the name of the Church. Certainly the Christian Church does not think of identifying its destiny with any victory this or that bloc may achieve. It counts among its members native churches in China, in India, in Africa. It does not believe in a biological Christianity that would be no more than an expression of the white man's morality. But the Church remembers that it has known glorious victories and tragic reverses that coincided with the fortunes of arms. The Saxons and the Mexicans had to choose between conversion and death. They preferred conversion, and so Germany and Mexico are Christian. On the other hand, the disciples of Mahomet presented the North Africans with a similar ultimatum; as a result, the Church lost one of its fairest provinces, the homeland of Saint Augustine. Again, the Church, knowing that God cannot be saved by force of arms, nevertheless holds that certain political regimes which guarantee the Church its physical existence are to be defended in preference to regimes that persecute the Church. It happens that the regimes which protect the Church are in the West. It is part of the Christian's duty, therefore, to put himself at the disposal of the Western armies. Thus the cold war of today and the hot war of tomorrow will assume the aspect of a religious war. Is it not a question, sociologically speaking, of a struggle between two social blocs, of which one, by and large, is on the side of the light, while the other represents darkness? Realizing as we do, we the wise and the intelligent, that everything is relative in the eyes of the Church, is it not an urgent necessity to call on the Christian West to furbish its arms in preparation for the crusade against the antichrist? Whole truth for the people, certainly, half-truth for the Church, but a half-truth which alone will permit us to insure the physical survival of the Christian society, and therefore of the ecclesiastical institution, and of the truth itself which it is the mission of that institution to embody on the earth.

We wish to make a point here of protesting strongly against this Machiavellian attitude prevalent in the Church today. We have more respect for the unvarnished sincerity of the atheists who hold that there is no truth outside society. A Church which disguises the supra-human truth it claims to teach beneath the hypocritical garment of half-truths acceptable to the people, in order to utilize the people in the service of temporal causes, to exploit their naïveté and their thirst for sacrifice, for the maintenance of a regime that protects ecclesiastical institutions, such a Church places itself under the terrible judgment of the God of truth who is its head. Eternal truth will not perish, but the Church will perish in contradictions. Many believers today raise a cry of alarm. It is a lie to say that the conflict between East and West is the struggle of darkness against light. If it is true that the laws of parliamentary regimes safeguard the liberty of the individual, it is equally true that the Marxist revolution tries to abolish the exploitation of one man by another—an imperfect effort perhaps, but one which can be the beginning of a juster regime, while the free enterprise of Western peoples involves the risk of prolonging without hope the exploitation of the backward peoples held down by the white man. If there is a split between the East and the West, it is wrong to say that all the light is on one side and all the shade on the other. We do not deny the dark sides, aspects which are horrible even, of Soviet totalitarianism, but, if it is the duty of the Church to denounce evil, wherever it may be, it is not the Church's place to preach a crusade against it, or to take part in such a crusade. Leave to Caesar what is Caesar's and to God what is God's.

Second hypothesis: truth is not of this world. It remains for us to examine the unquestioning acceptance of the teaching of Jesus concerning the nature of truth. Truth, he said, is not of this world; but, as he came to bear witness to this suprahuman truth his calm before Pilate is total. For the time being, Pilate has power over Jesus—is not the temporal power in his hands?—but in the final analysis it is truth that will judge Pilate and those who have delivered Jesus to him. Already Pilate is judging himself, for he knows he is condemning an innocent man. Societies likewise climb, prosper and rise to heaven like towers of Babel. They trample under foot the rights of man, scorn God and destroy human life. It matters little. They are already judged. They carry within themselves their own condemnation. The empires, the civilizations that have despised divine values will perish and be replaced by juster societies. The man who believes these things fears no longer for the future of truth. Truth laughs at human attempts to kill her. She is born afresh from the ashes of the stake. That is the message the Church should bring again to the world. It was always the message of the prophets, the apostles, the martyrs. It is senseless advising Christians to put their trust in anything but the eternal truth. It is equally illusory to devote ourselves blindly to the defense of existing social forms, or to throw ourselves into pseudo-revolutionary struggles. No army will save a society that has revolted against God. No revolution will triumph if it uses unrighteous methods. Human duty consists in serving unfalteringly in all circumstances, within conservative or revolutionary periods, the eternal truth which judges societies and individuals and will one day emerge triumphant. By acting thus, the true servant of his country, his people, his civilization, or of the revolution he may hold necessary, will accelerate the movement of history toward the approaching justice. On the other hand, every act of compromise with the emotions of the crowd or the errors of the state hastens divine judgment on them, and contributes to their final ruin.

We are not, however, going to allow ourselves to slip into the apocalyptic myth in which so many Christian sects take sad delight: The world is in the hands of the devil, let us be among the little flock of the elect. In fact, it is beyond question that humanity's march toward justice, however painful it may be, has meaning. We are not abandoning our deep confidence in the validity of human life. The societies around us have, in the course of history, gathered and embodied in the form of laws and customs more than a fragment of the order desired by God. The preaching of total anarchy does a great deal of harm to the truth. The established order must be respected, and opposed only in so far as it represents the negation of eternal truth. The sources of morality and religion, Henri Bergson has told us, are different. Let us give up trying to rationalize the universe. Let us stop declaring *all is matter* or *all is God*. Let us not be more systematic than the Bible, which from the very first lines distinguishes chaos and spirit. God, it says, moved over the chaos, seeking to penetrate and to organize it. God would be no more than disembodied perfection if he had not matter against him as an obstacle (but also providing him with a fulcrum for his levers), if matter was not in his hands like clay to be molded.

Matter, too, without God is nothing but a chaos where swirling eddies turn ever aimlessly upon themselves. So too, social whirlwinds are meaningless unless God intervenes to endow them with his order. Yet we should not allow religious idealism to lead us to deny that human societies are the point of resistance and leverage indispensable to God for his action on matter.

The burning interest of the drama of our existence comes from this fact. Any attempt to rationalize the universe with the object of reducing it to a philosophical or theological unity and of making Matter and Good one, is foredoomed to failure. A healthy, empirical recognition of the duality of Matter and Good, on the other hand, places us in an honest and quickening setting. Unity is not given in advance. It is for us to achieve it in our flesh and in our spirit. Without underestimating the complexity of the tension in which we live, it is our part as men to believe that it can be ended. If the individual is unable, with the stroke of a magic wand, to simplify the outside world, he can at the very least in faith find an inward unity. His reunified personality will react constructively on other personalities and so contribute to the ultimate unification of the world. Thus our faith embodies itself in untiring, always renewed attempts to transform our complex, imperfect world and to lead it to unity.

Chapter 6

God or Gods?

Is THE UNIVERSE A STAGE WHERE, AS THE GODS IN AN-
cient tragedy, contradictory principles clash with one another, cooperate, knot and untie themselves: light and
shade, life and death, time and space, good and evil,
justice and love, war and peace, pure beauty and blind
destiny? The ancients believed it was, the Hindus think
so today: as we contemplate its cycles, its struggles, its
illusions, the universe affords us intellectual, aesthetic and
mystical delights constantly renewed; but one day the
majestic rounds will cease, and all will become one again.
Christians and Orientals debate whether the ultimate
unity is a person or the liberation of all personal life.

The Bible, no less than other sacred books, traces a
similar fresco of the world: creation emerging from the
primeval unity has differentiated the elements. The Fall
has set man against God. But after the divine plan of redemption has been accomplished, unity will be restored
by a judgment which will eliminate all that is contrary to
God.

Such is the substratum of the teaching of the Bible, and of the higher religions. But while most of the religions stop at a philosophical explanation of the universe in the form of a few transparent symbols, and confine themselves to teaching their adherents submission to their destiny, moral purity and the spirit of sacrifice, combined with zeal for their forms of worship, the Bible, from the third chapter onward, abandons all philosophy. The event of the Fall of man leads all other events—cosmic, historical, religious—through the narrow gate of a doctrine simple in the extreme: good vs. evil. God is holy, man must be holy like him. The sole cause of the tragedy of the world, of man's forced labor and woman's suffering in childbirth, of pain and death, is human sin.

Meanwhile, Almighty God manifests his power in the world in two ways only: he punishes all individual or collective disobedience and he selects from among men and peoples those he wishes to make instruments of his Will.

All this is very simple and very arbitrary. There is no attempt in it at a philosophical explanation of the universe.

A significant number of phenomena defy classification in so elementary a scheme. But—and it is this that permits the view that the biblical paradox is not a product of man's imagination, but was revealed—while religions strive in vain to console man and explain his place in nature to him, the Bible is content to show man what God is for him, and to teach him plainly what he should be for God. It is the revelation of a Father, and of the way that leads to him. Nothing more.

Certainly there are many obscure passages in the Bible. The holy God seems unjust in his choices. He selects men and peoples who are not always holy. Nevertheless he uses them as witnesses. The demi-gods, Lucifer, the Baals, Beelzebub, Satan, the heavenly spirits, continue to play parts of secondary importance. Jesus believed in evil spirits, and Saint Paul in celestial authorities ("exousias"). How complicated all this is!

And how difficult it is to reconcile the ritual massacres God demanded of his people with the Sermon on the Mount. Yet all evasion of the essentially ethical revelation which dominates the Bible, every attempt to take refuge in these obscure passages, is a betrayal of Jesus. He is the lens which reduces all the many-colored rays of the Bible fresco to white light, and to the unity of a moral revelation. Theologians throw confusion into biblical interpretation the moment they deny the teaching and sacrifice of Jesus their unique place at the center of revelation. At this point we declare our unshakable belief in the unique role of Jesus Christ who, having fulfilled the Old and the New Testaments, alone can reveal their meaning to us. His is the right to tell us what the Old Testament and Saint John and Saint Paul and Saint Peter and the book of Revelation mean. He has not to be judged by them. We do not have to ask the disciples: Who, then, was the Master? Was he right, or did he oversimplify? We must go to the Master himself. His personality is so powerful that it shines through all the writings of the disciples. It is for him to tell us what their teaching is worth. It is a mistake to wonder if the Sermon on the Mount, preached by Jesus, is "Pauline" enough. It is rather Saint Paul who must be passed through the sieve of the Sermon on the Mount, and we must ask ourselves if his teaching is "Christian" enough. It is not for the Church to judge

Jesus; it is for Jesus to judge and reform the Church.

Now a serious examination of the Bible shows it to be a "Christian" book. The fringes of its teaching are secondary aspects. Satan still exists in the background. His activity cannot be denied, but he is no longer an accessory of God. He is only a beaten enemy. Jesus does not permit us to worship him, nor in any way to recognize his authority. The "authorities" described by Saint Paul bow before the Lord and are only humble instruments which he breaks, as he breaks the rebellious individual as soon as he turns away from him. Wanting to build a "theology" of the state on one half of the thirteenth chapter of the epistle to the Romans means abandoning the "axis" of the revelation, which passes exclusively through the three revealed aspects of God—Father, Son and Holy Spirit—and adds nothing to them. Let us be careful. With the aid of marginal texts of the Bible, a fourth "person" can readily be added to the Trinity: the Church, the State, the Race, Democracy, the Proletariat, Freedom, Humanity, Peace, the Human Person, and what not? Saint Paul is certainly profound in the thoughts he offers us, recognizing as he does the gravity of sin, the seriousness of the divine law, and the radical condemnation of all men. Against this somber background he strikes a dialectical balance between divine grace and justification by faith. It is good news which rejoices our hearts, but the problem remains: *Is Saint Paul a Christian?* That is to say, is he merely a religious philosopher who weighs the shadow and light of sin and grace in the majestic picture of the human drama he traces for us, or does he believe in the unique fact which has reversed the course of history: the incarnation, the teaching, the miracles, the atoning sacrifice and the physical resurrection of Jesus, and the gift of the Holy Spirit? Does he confess a God who has put an end to the dialectical movement of "semper peccator, semper justus" (always sinning, always just), and who brings the believer to his knees in the faith that all things are possible to those who believe?

We would be dishonest to refuse Saint Paul the title of Christian, to refuse to recognize in him a humble disciple of Jesus, a modest explainer of his teaching, and a teacher himself who has added nothing to, nor taken anything away from, the Sermon on the Mount, the parables, the final discourses of Holy Week, and who strove ceaselessly to demonstrate the full reality of the transformation brought about by the Savior in the world: henceforth every man in faith can follow in the footsteps of Jesus because, reborn, he receives his Spirit. The world itself, according to Saint John, Saint Paul and Saint Peter, as an object of divine grace loved by God, will ultimately be created anew after having passed through the fire. Thus, for Saint Paul, for the prophets, for the apostles and for Jesus, dialectical reasoning comes *before* the redeeming act and not after it. The Cross of Jesus marks a *final* event in the middle of history. By it, Jesus reduces all things to unity. After it, there is nothing but God triumphing over evil.

The Christian is a warrior who receives his arms and orders with the certainty of victory. He no longer allows the spectacle of chaos in the world or its internal disorders to deter him. He is a man who has taken sides, but not as a philosopher. His side is the side of Jesus Christ. He stands alone in the midst of the world's complexities, but in his solitude he is more aware of history, more loving toward his country, closer to all men, than is the philosopher, because he bears them witness to a Savior who is there, near to them in the present, able to deliver them now. Jesus Christ, unifier and organizer of the world, is in the final analysis its only explanation. Men will never explain the world by studying its origins or analyzing its present condition. It can be explained only in terms of the end toward which it is moving. Since Jesus, a perfectly straight axis has pierced the chaos like an arrow. It is only a stroke in the tumultuous mass, a straight line amid the whirling eddies. But everything must be set in order according to this axis. Henceforth no human life can have its meaning explained except in terms of the absolute perfection that Jesus assigns to it as its goal. The world will dash itself to pieces on this rock, or rebuild with it as cornerstone. Let the Church become Christian, let its members become disciples of Christ, and everything will be illuminated. The disorders and agonies of humanity will become meaningful. They are only birth pangs. A woman is ready to endure the greatest pain; she despairs only when her suffering is to no end. In Jesus Christ no suffering is without purpose.

For centuries Christian theology taught these things, but it gave way more and more to a desire to systematize. Theologians became systematic and summarized the Bible in a few logical propositions. After the fixing of Catholic dogma came the Protestant rationalism of the right, with its rigid "ordo-salutis," then the rational theism of the left in the 18th century, then the experimental sentimentalism of the pietists, and finally, with the birth of the psychological and sociological sciences, the theologians set about reducing the Bible to a handful of general laws applicable to man and society.

Reaction was inevitable. Modern dialectical theology escapes from the hold of the rationalisms by giving up all idea of explaining biblical revelation. It is at the moment, it says, when man abandons his attempt to grasp God by reason, at the moment when he accepts the divine mystery as impenetrable, that God speaks to him. The word of God is not logical. It is double, paradoxical, in form. His imperatives are not fixed; they vary according to circumstances.

We owe a large debt of gratitude to the dialectical theologians; they have led us out of the blind alley where the rationalists of right and left had confined us. But they have landed themselves today in a new quandary. At a moment when the Christian world, and the world at large, looks to its spiritual leaders for guidance matching the problems of the day—capitalism, communism, fascism—theology is silent. The note its trumpet sounds is not clear. Why? Because theology finds itself unable to derive moral conclusions from dialectical reasoning. The dialectical method is an excellent instrument of analysis, but in its present form it breaks down before the synthesis. For the sublime appeals of the Sermon on the Mount and the precise commandments of Jesus, it substitutes casuistry: "In such and such a circumstance God may require such and such an attitude. No attitude is perfect. The will of God is made known sometimes by prophetic means, sometimes through the state as guardian of the order willed by God."

Let us beware. Casuistry has always marked periods of moral laxity and decadence in the Church.

Let us be clear, too. The dialectical method introduced by Hegel was not limited to a ceaseless oscillation between two opposites. When thesis and antithesis have been stated, Hegel thought that the contradiction could be resolved by a synthesis situated on a higher plane.

The Marxists have retained the Hegelian method, not in its logical form. It is in life that the conflict between the thesis and the antithesis will be resolved. A society better adapted to the present economic order will take the place of antiquated social, moral and religious forms, which are condemned by the march of history. Marxist dialectic is thus extraordinarily dynamic; it creates the vision of a world inevitably transformed to become more just. Christians of the early centuries looked forward to and prepared with similar fervor for the coming of the Messiah's kingdom.

Ah, if only dialectical theology led to a synthesis, what power it would have in thought, what dynamic inspiration for Christians in action. We hope, we believe, that this splendid mother will soon bear a child worthy of herself, proclaiming to the world the new synthesis of justice and love. The day must come when Christians reunited will declare to the world that there is a clearly formulated Christian duty, and only one, since there is only one God, one Savior, one baptism. But for the moment the quest for a synthesis is most curiously regarded by certain theologians as the sin of sins. All syntheses are rejected, those of the right and those of the left, and more seriously, the synthesis of Jesus Christ himself. God hides himself, they say, forgetting it was not God who hid from man after the Fall, but man who is ever seeking to escape from the sight of God, whose eye is too pure for him.

Saint Paul himself declares that the invisible perfection of God, his eternal power and his divinity are seen as with the naked eye. Where then is the "deus abscond-itus"? Jesus came. "Whoever has seen me," he said, "has seen the Father." Where does Jesus demand the believer's surrender to a dialectical mystery? Where does he suggest that we tread fearfully between two evils, obliged always to choose the lesser? Certainly there are many things my reason cannot grasp. I know that God loves me and yet judges me, that he offers me grace when I know I am hopelessly sinful; yet his grace delivers me completely from sin. I know he is the Lord of history, but leaves man his freedom; that his will requires a society founded on love, but that he desires also the maintenance of the social order.

But all these things are theses and antitheses which herald and lead up to *the* synthesis: Jesus Christ.

All this precedes Jesus Christ; it does not come after him. It announces the synthesis; it does not destroy it. If there were a dialectic and if it still exists for those who live today *before* Jesus Christ, this dialectic is an intimate drama belonging to God himself *before* the historic fact of the Cross. "To punish or to pardon?" he debates through the mouths of the prophets. But the day when justice and forgiveness unite on the Cross, they bring forth the divine sacrifice. The synthesis on the higher plane has been realized. After Jesus Christ and in the hope of his imminent return, nothing remains for the believer but to tread, in perfect faith, the way open before him: the way of Jesus, of the Sermon on the Mount, of the parables, of the prayer in Gethsemane, of the Cross,

of the resurrection of Jesus who gives himself to us
through the Holy Spirit.

It is tragic to see theology, in its denial of the moral
character of God and of his revelation, cutting the ground
from under its own feet and destroying itself. In its desire
to avoid the "gnoses," it risks reducing itself to the role
of a "gnosis." The entire Bible is built up on a moral
order given to man: "Thou shalt not eat of the forbidden
fruit." There was nothing to prevent its being obeyed.
Even after the Fall, God maintained his requirement:
"Be ye holy as I am holy, be ye perfect as your Father in
heaven is perfect." Moral obligation cannot tolerate dialectic. If men ought to do good but cannot, the word
"ought" becomes meaningless. Its meaning has been
changed, we are told, by the corruption of the human
race; the "ought" of "thou shalt" remains, but no longer
as an order, only a judgment. Let us admit it. But then
God's arm must be too short to save. If God's arm is too
short to save, something is lacking in his perfection. If
God is not perfect, the redeeming sacrifice was a fine
gesture, bloody and of no avail. If redemption remains
without effect, there is no more moral obligation, only
dialectical hesitation between a number of possibilities,
all equally mediocre. The Christian's moral duty is reduced to casuistical oscillation between several evils. God,
it is said, covers that with the veil of his infinite compas-
sion. Certainly! That's what we mean by God. But this
God is no longer the God of the prophets and Jesus
Christ, terror of demons and savior of the penitent. This
theology is no longer the theology of salvation, it is an ill-
defined branch of knowledge, an interesting series of
snapshots of the divinity taken from different angles. God

has been taken apart and they cannot put the pieces together again. His power, his justice, his mercy, his honor, his kingdom, his providence, his order, his love, all are in conflict with each other. They are found embodied almost everywhere: in the Father, Son and Holy Spirit, certainly, but also in the churches and the states, and the wars of the Old Testament (and perhaps those of today as well), not forgetting the sacraments and history, which the inscrutable God directs in his mysterious way. The East has naturalized God; the West tries, with little success, not to utilize him for its own profit. But the one that everybody has tamed is the devil. Since God uses him as a necessary aid to his triumph, he must be served in passing, mustn't he?

Without such a synthesis, which is moral as well as theological, Christianity will dissolve into a new polytheism. The God of Jesus Christ will be replaced by the gods of former times—Jupiter, Minerva, Mars, Mercury —unless these are already, under different names, the gods of today.

Civilizations cannot be founded on a dialectic. They can be built only on the cornerstone. Jesus Christ in saving us will restore moral obligation. Either the Church will rediscover its faith in the gospel synthesis, or else fall in ruins together with our crumbling world. Then from the East and from the West will come Marxists and fascists to impose their elementary systems on a world that is too complicated. And the Church, under persecution, will repent. But it would be better if it repented now, while it is influential and respected.

Part Three

THE "FOURTH" DIMENSION

Chapter 7

The Politics of Repentance

Politics, we are told, is the art of living in society. Social life proceeds on the economic plane (physical existence), on the cultural plane (intellectual and artistic existence) and on the moral plane (religious existence). Now here is this society of which I form part and from which I cannot separate myself, this society which lives by me and by which I am enabled to live.

This society is constantly faced with threats to its existence. It is threatened, first, by internal decay: disease and death, cultural decline, moral laxity. It is threatened equally from without, by rival societies ready to overwhelm and absorb it, by a nation or a race challenging it, by a more prosperous economic or stronger military regime, by a more vital religion. This is as true for the church as it is for the nation.

It is necessary, then, for this society to which I belong and for which I obviously have my share of responsibility, to defend itself, like any living organism, against internal decay and external dangers. And if I think of "society-as-it-ought-to-be" instead of "society-as-it-is," I do not rad-ically alter the problem, for on the one hand the future society must defend itself, for the same reasons, from the present society, and on the other, the future exists already as a germ in the present, and I know I must be careful not to kill the hen that is to lay tomorrow's egg.

I write all this with a sense of warm admiration for those who work with the realities of the physical dimension, the "homo economicus": the farmer first and foremost, the productive worker, the engineer, the administrator, the railwayman and the sailor who risks his life bringing the necessities of life to others. I would admire the magistrate, the policeman, the governor, the soldier and the officer, who defend the order of society. I would applaud the doctor, the surgeon, the nurse, who save human beings in danger. I would respect the teacher, the professor, the scholar, the artist, who raise the child up from its animal nature to cultivate its intelligence and enrich its life. If I belong to the most highly developed of men, I would applaud the priests and the pastors who crown man with honor by teaching him the "you ought," revealing to him the world of love and sacrifice. These people form the very substance of life in society; they are the cells of a living tissue which ought to defend itself. Now it happens that, even if I do not go to church, I am a Christian, and that the nations of the West, where I was born, as a whole constitute a Christendom which, though torn too often by internal wars, remains singularly vigorous and homogeneous, its parts stoutly cemented by a common religion and a common morality. I wish for the whole world that it may one day be Christianized. Perhaps not in a narrow confessional sense, but certainly under the noble discipline of the teaching of Jesus. This will not come about of its own accord. There will be struggles and suffering, successes and reverses; millions of men will have to pledge themselves and their responsibility in the battle; thousands must be prepared consciously and voluntarily to sacrifice their lives. The notion of a world without purpose must be rejected, then, as cowardly and illusory.

Our problem is to know what form of struggle, what method we are to adopt.

First method of defense: preserving the container. The first form of struggle I will define as: preserving the container to safeguard the contents. If a fragile glass bottle containing a precious liquid is broken, the liquid is lost. So I shall protect the bottle with straw cushions. In the case of a society, I shall build around it a Maginot line, or since such fortifications are out of date, I shall establish, as far from its nerve center as possible, a network of sea and air bases; I shall see that it has a sufficient supply of raw materials, strategic and non-strategic; I shall endeavor to develop markets for its trade; I shall train its youth for war, not forgetting intellectual and moral armaments, to prevent the infection by doubt of souls always prone to egoism; I shall construct a logical system of reasoning around the truth that is to be defended, mobilize the press, the radio, the schools, and above all the Church. Then I shall go to bed, satisfied I have done my bit toward organizing the defense of my truth, in peace as in war.

Alas, the truth, if it be Christian, will die by starvation behind the bars of such a prison! In my concern for the container, I am very apt to discover when the bottle is uncorked that the precious fluid has lost its fragrance, and that I have given myself a great deal of trouble for nothing.

Second method of defense: the Church's method. In the course of history the Church has developed as "a society within society," a specialized society whose function is not economic, intellectual or artistic, but essentially moral and religious. Here we must recall the distinction drawn by Bergson. As a moral and religious institution, the Church's role is conservative. It transmits to future generations a knowledge of religious truth and an example of pure morals. Everything noble the past has left us will command its sympathy. It was not by chance that the Church became the protector and servant of kings, who, it taught the people, were appointed by God. It is not by chance that today the Church is alarmed every time the traditional forms of duty are called into question. It knows from experience that it is easy to leave the well-sheltered roads for explorations on the high seas, but difficult to bring back to port the ship of opinion that has lost its bearings and lies at the mercy of the four winds of heaven. That is why the Church is cautious, excessively cautious, even with the prophets who arise in its midst.

But, says Bergson, there is the other source of morality and religion. The Church itself is prophetic. It is not only entrusted with transmitting a tradition. It is on its knees to receive inspiration from on high, to receive orders that are revolutionary. That is why the Church celebrates the sacraments. The Catholic church has seven of them, the Protestant church retains two: the sacrament of baptism, which makes it possible, by cleansing a man with pure water, to begin again with him the whole of human history by relieving him of hereditary corruption; and communion, which reproduces in us the regeneration brought about by the sacrifice of Jesus, nourishing us with the substance of his life and heralding the new society of the kingdom of God. Wherever the sacraments are celebrated, human life is penetrated by the divine absolute. Everything is taken up again from the beginning. No discouragement, no pessimism, no compromise is fitting when we are plunged into the liberating grace of God. Alas, practice has worn out the effectiveness of the sacraments. The Church knows that the faith of its members is indispensable if the sacraments are to be effective. But the faith of the members is poor. It has gradually deteriorated into belief, adhesion to an intellectual formula, and then into superstition, or confidence in the automatic effects of objects, words and sacred ceremonies. The Church has lost its living contact with the Beyond and its prophetic character. It remains attached to the sacraments, and it is well that it does so. It holds that through them, in spite of the weakness of our faith, something divine is transmitted to the world. Nevertheless, when faith becomes weak it tends to be replaced by institutions, and around the sacrament arises a sanctuary in which to celebrate it. A clergy is constituted to administer it, for holy matters cannot be entrusted to just anybody. The clergy organize themselves into a hierarchy because sacred doctrines are not determined by majority vote in a democratic assembly. From the beginning, the transmission of the apostolic teaching was confided to "faithful men, capable of teaching also to others." This was the origin of the apostolic succession, then of the papacy.

Around the sacrament the Church organized itself as a powerful institution. History has proved that it could weather storms, even when apparently beaten; the church, so long as it remained true to itself, continued the ministry of Jesus upon earth. Thus on the religious plane, a human society is formed and the defense of the "container," which is the Church, must be assured in order to save the contents: the doctrine of divine intervention in human affairs through the medium of the sacraments. The Church, however, has a superiority over races and nations. It is no longer identified with a people as it was in the time of Israel. It is dispersed among the nations; it is a spiritual society that no longer coincides with any sociologically defined group. So it seems that it should be able to rise above ideological conflicts and international wars. These, as the Church should understand, belong to the domain of the relative. The only conflict which interests the Church is the struggle between God and the forces of evil.

All this is true in theory, but we have just described the evolution by which the Church became a human society owing itself survival, physical survival, for the sake of preserving the truth it embodies. Consecrated sanctuaries, religious schools for the instruction of the young, monasteries for prayer, property for livelihood, laws for protection, bonds linking national churches with the Vatican —none of these things can be held cheap. So the Church finds itself obliged to engage in politics in order to defend its constitution, its teaching, its schools, its property. Yet the Church's politics are different from the State's: the Church is more discriminating. The Church does not spill blood. Its attitude will vary according to the kind of State it has to deal with. If the State protects the Church, the State is accorded the privilege of being recognized as a Catholic state, and the Church supports it without reserve, even if its regime is totalitarian. If a democratic state gives the Church the same guarantees as it accords to every non-subversive group of citizens, the Church will grant it its approval. It will recommend the faithful to serve the State in peace and in war. It will expect in return the good offices of the State. It will even allow itself to intervene in internal politics with the object of obtaining laws favorable to its educational ministry. But if the State, on the other hand, threatens the ministry and influence of the Church, closes church schools, prohibits public collections, teaches anti-Christian morals or beliefs, dispossesses the religious orders, expels missionaries, endeavors to break the links between the national clergy and the Vatican, then the Church resists, and its priests are deported, its bishops stand trial.

We admire these martyrs who suffer and die for the Church. Yet certain aspects of this struggle disturb us: Is it really the struggle of faith against the powers of darkness? The indulgence, not to say more, of the Church toward certain immoral regimes which protect it seems scandalous in the eyes of many Catholics. If tomorrow this or that government, today a persecutor, found that it would be to its advantage to offer the Church a compromise, and guaranteed it an honorable place in the heart of the revolutionary society, is it not probable that the Church would accept the reconciliation? Such is the extent to which it is true to say that the Church does not determine its attitude toward regimes according to their virtues or their crimes, but according to the favors or dis-

favors received from them. Defense of the ecclesiastical
institution has therefore taken precedence over the defense of Christianity. The prophetic ministry of the
Church has been displaced by church politics.

Let the Protestant not boast overmuch either. If it is
true that in the past Protestant countries have assured
themselves liberal constitutions, it is none the less evident
that the lack of a centralizing authority has allowed the
national Protestant churches to become as completely
subject as the church of Rome to the policies of their re-
spective governments. If tomorrow a holy crusade were
to be launched, it would be preached, I fear, in the
churches of all confessions with the same blind zeal.
Nevertheless, important differences separate the Catholics
and the Protestants on this point.

Third method of defense: the Word of God. The
Protestant churches differ from the Roman Catholic
church in the importance they attach to the reading and
interpreting of the Word of God. The Protestant church
depends for its existence on a constant return to Christian
origins. True, sacramental and institutional features are
not absent from the life of Protestant communities. We
are even witnessing a reaction in this respect, and a certain rapprochement with the Catholic position. But the
essential characteristic of the Protestant church still remains its preaching, that is, the faithful explanation of
God's Word by the minister, in its purity, its severity and
its forgiveness. On Saturday, as he prepares his sermon,
the preacher submits himself to the harsh discipline of the
Scriptures. He does not ask himself, "How does the
Church explain this passage?", but rather, "What has
this passage to say to the Church, what does it say to

me?" Often he emerges broken from this struggle. Then his preaching is God's instrument which, in turn, breaks the believers. The believer comes to church to be judged and lifted up by the divine word. He goes back home after a rough examination of conscience, but rejoicing because he has received pardon and the strength to do better.

It is here that the Protestant's difficulties begin. While the Catholic belongs to a disciplined institution which prescribes a clearly defined line of conduct for its members and gives them absolution for all that remains undefined or unsolved in their problems, the Protestant is sent home alone in the presence of God, that is, alone with his conscience. He is a workman, a farmer, a tradesman, a manufacturer, a civil servant, a magistrate, a soldier. His function in society gives him "duties of state," that is, conscientious and loyal service to his nation or his social group. But his position as a Christian means that he also has the duty of unconditional obedience to the Gospel, where the commandment of holiness is clear and unmistakable to him: "Be ye perfect as your Father in heaven is perfect." A painful tension, sometimes almost unbearable, is created. It transforms the sincere Protestant into a being tormented with anxiety. This is especially true at the age of adolescence. Young students of theology, young seekers of the absolute in youth groups, dream of breaking with the world. Every new Protestant sect has its origin in a courageous attempt to revive the primitive church in true faithfulness to the Word of God. Calvin at Geneva attempted nothing else. But life undertakes to train the Protestant. He cannot, as the Catholic, resort to entering a religious order. His thirst for the absolute cannot be quenched. He will marry, he will earn his living more or less easily, he will have children, he will be concerned with their careers, he will concentrate all his conscientious enthusiasm on his family life and his duties as a citizen. He will continue to go to church. He will often criticize his minister, accusing him of being in the clouds, of knowing nothing about life, of having no sense of reality. In point of fact, since the end of the period of "revivals" and their insistent calls to repentance, since theologians have discovered the tragic character of a world that does not lend itself readily to reformation in accordance with Gospel principles, ministers have become wiser. Their Bible commentaries are dialectical; often they shrink even from preaching on Gospel texts. They have made the tension between law and grace, justice and love, the particular object of their studies. The result is that the Protestant churches are adapting themselves better than ever to the world. In so doing, they are betraying their true nature as churches of reformation, not of the historical Reformation, which belongs to the past, but of a continuous reformation wrought by the Word of God itself.

What has this reformation been? Has it been a portrait of our inner conflicts? Surely not! So long as Luther, tormented with anxiety, inflicted even harsher penances on himself in his monastic cell, there was no Reformation. But it was released the moment he rediscovered the scriptural truth that "the just shall live by faith." So long as George Fox traveled about England, fasting, praying and meditating, his painful search remained sterile. But when at the age of 22 he received his vision of "the ocean of darkness and death of our world, covered by an infinite ocean of light and divine love," it was the beginning of a powerful movement the effects of which are still not exhausted. So long as John Wesley, consumed by inner conflict, wandered lost among the ways of asceticism and ritualism, his zeal bore no fruit. It was only at the age of 35, during an ethical meeting, that he felt "his heart strangely warmed" and put his trust in Christ alone for his salvation. The following year saw the beginning of his open-air missions which were to transform the England of the 18th century. It is possible that the tension that is growing in the churches and in Christian theology today heralds a return to the Word of God, a movement of total faith in the power of God to forgive us and to render us capable of doing good; but in any case, the systematization of this tension in the form of a teaching that would have us believe Christian morality is a choice between two different forms of evil, that the Sermon on the Mount will remain inapplicable on earth until the final coming of Christ; in any case, such teaching cannot be the mark of a faithful Church reforming itself constantly according to the Word of God.

Fourth method of defense: purity. This is certainly the most religious and the most moral means of defending the truth, perhaps the only method that is genuinely moral and religious. Is it not God's own method? Ever since man began his struggle against God, against His total purity, striving to kill him, God's sole defense has been to remain nothing but total purity. An absolutely paradoxical fact with the gift of exasperating the atheist. Nowhere can man have experience of perfection; he finds it neither in nature, nor in society, nor in the church nor in himself. Yet the notion of absolute perfection never leaves him. It besets him, as Job says, "during his nights." So we have not to defend truth. We have to become aware of it, accept its evidence. We have to embody it, reveal it to others. The perfection of our lives will be its defense. People are not mistaken when they expect the Church to shine, not by the splendor of its ceremonies, the power of its thinking, the multiplicity of its good works, but through the saintliness of its representatives. Instinctively they expect Christians to be better than others; if they are the same, people are scandalized. Jesus, moreover, agrees with the people when he tells us: "Except your righteousness shall exceed the righteousness of the scribes and Pharisees, ye shall in no case enter into the kingdom of heaven."

So truth's perfection is its only defense, and if we desire truth to be spread and upheld in the world, we must be perfect in the world.

The world habitually lies? The Christian will always tell the truth. The world is immoral? The Christian's conduct will be pure. The world cheats and exploits? The Christian does not steal, but shares his goods. The world slanders? The Christian blesses. The world returns evil for evil? The Christian does not resist the evildoer. The world kills? The Christian saves. The world seeks to end aggression and exploitation by war? The Christian will begin with himself. He will prefer the risk of being killed to killing, of being exploited to exploiting, of being deceived to deceiving. And what is "worst" in this method of defense, so discouraging in its simplicity, is that it is the good way, the only true way, and therefore the only effective way. All the stratagems described in the three preceding sections end by turning against the truth it was their purpose to save, since they are all, in the last resort, negative in character.

Alas, over against the evidence we must set the experience. The popular proverb, which has nothing biblical about it, *"Qui veut faire l'ange fait la bête"* (He who seeks to make an angel makes a beast) is tragically true. The man who sets out to be perfect, who eliminates one by one all his faults, is visited by the supreme fault, pride: "God, I thank thee that I am not as other men are." Jesus, after commanding us to be perfect, is extremely severe with the perfectionists of his time, the Pharisees, who, he says, "cannot be justified by God because they give themselves their own reward on earth."

So, through fear of pride, the supreme sin against God, against men and against oneself, the Church as an educator of great experience has abandoned the doctrine of perfection. It reserves it only very exceptionally for its saints. It prudently warns its flock of the danger that lurks in wanting to play the saint: "You want to be a conscientious objector, to refuse lying, compromise, exploitation, participation in war? Be careful, is that humility? Are you sure there is no passion in your heart, no secret thought, to disqualify you for this role? Are you not deceiving yourself? And again, even if you wanted to be pure, even if you *were* pure inwardly, your hands would still be stained with other men's blood. Interdependence makes you guilty. By eating you take the bread from another's mouth. By making a position for yourself you have a part in exploiting your brother, by refusing to fight you send another to be killed in your place, by refraining from liberating your country from the invader, or freeing oppressed peoples, you make yourself an accomplice of the torturers of the concentration camp. Be humble, then, you are not an angel; the kingdom of God will not appear on earth until the end of time. Accept your human condition; you are only one man among many. Play your insignificant part cheerfully. The choice you have to make is not between impossible perfection and crime, but between two relative imperfections. Choose the lesser evil; this is the highest level of honesty you can attain. God is able to forgive you the rest."

The abandonment of defense. How clear and reasonable all this is, in the geometry of our three human dimensions: the physical, the intellectual and the religious. It would all be obvious were it not for the fourth dimension, the dimension that defies description, the dimension of God—of Jesus Christ. Here is a God as clear as crystal. His Son, too, is of perfect transparency. Everything in the Old Testament, as well as in Jesus' parables, points to the future. His eyes are too pure to witness iniquity. None can endure before him. He is the negation of nothingness. So the judgment will take place. The rotten history of mankind is going to end. All men are guilty, the elect even more so than the rest. To fulfill the terrible prophecy, Caiaphas the High Priest, the Sadducees and the Pharisees, Pilate the governor, with his soldiers and his centurion, the fickle mocking crowd, Judas the traitor, Peter the renegade, and the fainthearted disciples, are going to conspire together to crucify the God whose eye is too pure. They will succeed so well that there can be only one result: the suicide of a world rejecting the cause of its existence. The earth is going to be purged in a cosmic catastrophe. But this is the moment at which the fourth dimension becomes manifest. God does not defend his purity, he capitulates. The whole world's shame is upon him. He accepts it, he takes it upon himself; there is a ghastly void. God has ceased to exist; there is no more purity, only a great emptiness, a bottomless pit of despair. Mankind awaits a punishment which does not come, a redressing of the balance, purity's revenge, which does not take place. Then comes the extraordinary Easter morning: the fourth dimension is revealed, death exists no more, punishment is swallowed up in victory. The world has been created a second time, mankind makes a fresh start, no hope is too great, in Christ. Evil holds sway no longer. It is a marvelous springtime.

And what is most extraordinary of all is that this ineffable fourth dimension is there for me and for all men; the gift of the Holy Spirit is proof of it, for it is the whole world that God has loved. I would escape from the cosmic rays of grace if I could, but I am powerless to do so. Even if I run away from my father's house, my father's loving concern follows me everywhere. I can only hate him, like the insolvent debtor who detests his creditor and dreams of killing him; or else return to the house which is always open, where a welcome awaits me that is "worse" than nonviolent, the welcome of love. Thus the necessary choice between perfection and crime is restored, but no longer on the moral and religious plane. Moral relativity is abolished and replaced by a new relationship of person to person, between God and myself. To grace I can answer only "yes" or "no."

The Christian Church is no more than each of its members, for there is consciousness only in the individual. It has no other reason for existing than to bear witness to the event we have just attempted to describe. In the geometry of our three dimensions, it has nothing more to teach us than any other higher religion. But in the order of grace its mission is unique in the world. Why unique? Because the Church—or Christians, it is the same thing— *possesses* no truth. The Church is not at the head of a doctrinal or social system which belongs to it and is therefore to be defended by it; the truth, or rather the divine person it has to interpret, can only be received. The Church's hands are always empty, it is always holding them out, always receiving. It can give only when it receives, and that is what constitutes its humility, its poverty, its nonviolence. Whenever it enriches itself, it betrays God and denies its true nature.

The Church has no frontiers to defend. It is not a party, not even the party of "the Good." Fear is unknown to it. It has no intellectual limits, no need to vindicate God. Its action is reduced to receiving the Holy Spirit. And every time it receives, it gives and imparts to those around it the joy of salvation.

We were saying earlier that this can be translated at once onto the political plane. We will take a recent example. Pastor Niemöller is well known as the animating spirit of the German resistance to Hitler. He refused to apply racial laws within the church, refused to allow the truth confessed by the church to be distorted under the influence of Nazi theories. His preaching was so courageous that Hitler had him interned at Dachau. There, his opposition to the National-Socialist regime, to the tortures it inflicted on the Jews, to the war it thrust upon the world, gradually increased. Then it became total. In ever-increasing numbers, the Germans turned to Niemöller. They hailed him as the man who had saved the honor of the church, and who in some measure would save the honor of Germany itself. He was thought of as tomorrow's religious leader (and, who knows, perhaps the political leader as well) of a Germany delivered from the brown plague. Then in 1945 Niemöller came out of prison. People waited for him to utter a resounding "Rally around me!" Is this not the man with clean hands, the clear-sighted patriot, and the true Christian? Niemöller is not a timid man. But now, instead of expressing his pride as a resister, he drew up, with the Bishop of Worms and the resistant church, a confession of his sins and of his share in the responsibility of his people for the crimes committed while he was in prison. As a result, Niemöller lost the sympathy of eighty per cent of the Germans who had sought shelter behind his innocence; but to the confessing church of Germany his act opened the gates of grace. Because of his repentance, the blessing of God lies over Germany today. God is glorified when man humbles himself.

But that is not all. Niemöller will certainly assure anyone who wants to know that he is not a pacifist. Why? Because, as a good Lutheran, he is afraid of substituting for the religion of grace a Pharisaic religion of works. Yet Niemöller and his friend, the former minister Heinemann, who resigned from the government on conscientious grounds, are opposing the remilitarization of their country, and for two essential reasons. The first is that the pardoned sinner does not go back to his old crime, in this case militarism. The second is that Niemöller is deeply convinced that the misfortunes of Germany have sprung from its lack of faith in God. Although he himself refuses to outline a "Christian" political program for his country, he believes that his role as a Christian in the midst of the present darkness is to commit his country in faith to the hands of God alone.

If there are no Christian politics, no "direct political application of the Sermon on the Mount," if there ought to be no church politics, no "ecclesiastical strategy aimed at preserving the divine institution," there is, nevertheless, determining the course of history, the repentance of the individual Christian, for himself, for his church, for his country. Such repentance has very definite consequences in the social and political order. The unfortunate thing is that the necessity of repentance and faith, and of the change of conduct thus made possible, becomes apparent to Christians only at times of defeat and humiliation. If only the Christians of the victorious countries were to follow Niemöller's example with the same deep consciousness of having sinned, the world's destiny would be transformed.

Who is guilty of the crimes of mankind? There certainly are guilty men. They must be judged by earthly courts. After the First World War, Germany, under compulsion, was obliged to admit unilateral guilt by signing the Treaty of Versailles. The verdict was partial. This forced confession poisoned the German soul and contributed greatly to the rise of Nazism. It was a case for the Germans of proving to themselves not only that they were not alone to blame for the war, not only that the guilt was shared, but indeed that they were totally innocent. Man is made that way. If he cannot resort to confessing his fault before God and his brethren, he must prove to himself and to others, by a method that is psychologically watertight, that the fault never existed, that he has always been right. Hitler answered to this need; the object of the Second World War was to wipe out the offense of Versailles and prove to the world that Germany was innocent!

After the second war, the Allies tried not to repeat the error of Versailles. They organized the Nuremberg trials and numerous other trials for war crimes. These trials were conducted fairly. The accused were able to avail themselves of all the usual guarantees granted to defendants. The idea was good. It had to be made plain to instigators of future wars that they would not go unpunished. The infliction of the death penalty on the Nazi criminals may be regretted, but the need for a sanction remains. Yet Nuremberg did not resolve two aspects of the problem of guilt before international law.

The first is this: the war criminals of the defeated countries have been tried, but not those of the victorious. In 1945 there was a unique opportunity for proclaiming the equality of all men before international law. Since the French Revolution, it has been known that for law to be effective and respected it must be applied without distinction to all citizens, whatever their rank, their fortune, or, we should say today, their country or their party. Failure to try, before the same court and in accordance with the same code, American, English, French and Russian war criminals has meant that the edifice of justice it was desired to erect has been caused to totter.

The poisoned seeds of new political myths, which may lead to a third world war, have been scattered on the earth. The first is the myth of unilaterally guilty peoples (in this case, Germany again, already straightening up to throw off its cloak of disgrace). The second myth is that

of innocent nations. We are not thinking here of France
(the French are not very proud of their fit of collabora-
tion) but of America and Russia. Here are two peoples
who remember having been unjustly attacked by Japan
and Germany, and whose military leaders, not having
been arraigned before a court of justice, are assumed to
be without fault. The Americans and the Russians, therefore, remain ignorant of atrocities of which they may
have made themselves guilty. They imagine themselves
two innocent peoples who have never sinned against
peace. So each interprets every move the other makes as
prejudicial to its own will to peace. Nothing more is
needed for the creation of moral conditions likely to lead
to a third war. People convinced of their own innocence
cannot be reconciled. Only the repentant can.

The second aspect of the problem of collective guilt of
which the war crimes tribunals were aware but did not
resolve—and can it be resolved by tribunals?—is the
question of knowing who is really guilty of the crime committed. Is it the commander who gives the order, Hitler
or some officer, is it the agent who carries out the order,
the "S.S.," the "Gestapo," is it the person who is impli-
cated as a witness of the crime, or a passive accomplice
(the soldier belonging to the guilty unit), or is it the clear-
sighted citizen who, knowing the abominable nature of the
act committed, contents himself with saying "What can I
do about it?" and allows it to happen? The problem is not
a new one. It occurred at the foot of the cross of Jesus
Christ. Who was guilty of the death of Jesus? Caiaphas
who suggested it, Pilate who consented and gave the
order for the execution, the soldier who drove in the nails,
the crowd that stood by mocking, the disciples, finally,

who alone were aware of the true nature of the drama being enacted and who allowed it to go on without intervening, Simon Peter?

The reply of our contemporary courts is that the leader is the guilty one. The reply of the Gospel is that the most guilty is the one who realizes most deeply what is taking place. If as Christians we accept this view, we cannot avoid the conclusion that the history of the world depends very much more on the Church than we would wish, and that the Church, possessing as it does the secret of repentance and faith, cannot maintain as Peter did when they were killing his neighbor: "I don't know the man." It is for the Christians of all countries to repent first on their own account, and to change their conduct without delay. The consequences of their act will be incalculable. There are, let us repeat, no Christian politics; but the repentance of Christians and the change of conduct that springs from it can profoundly modify the course of political events.

Chapter 8

The Church in Society

IT IS NOT POSSIBLE TO SPEAK USEFULLY OF THE CHRIS-
tian's duty in society without mentioning the Church. If it
is true that the Christian is torn between duty to God and
"duties of state," if it is true that some Christians have
had the courage to face alone, in the name of Jesus
Christ, the severities of human law, while the Church dis-
carded them or left them to their own devices, if it is true
that today the majority of the official churches still support conscientious objectors in principle only and often
challenge their point of view with a theology interlarded
with considerations of expedience, this situation is irregu-
lar; for in point of fact, the objectors are doing no more
than reminding the Church of its own vocation, and the
Church at bottom knows this. Realizing the absurdities of
the modern world and its mortal contradictions, it is
slowly and surely orientating itself toward a radical opposition to all war. We rejoice at these encouraging signs.

Much has been written on the relations betwen Church
and State in the past. There was a time when the Church

76

was one with the nation. Moses founded a theocratic state; he withdrew into the "tabernacle of the congregation" to receive God's orders, which he then transmitted to the people of whom he was political head, lawgiver and prophet at the same time. But Moses was not a priest. This function was reserved for his brother Aaron, whose concessions to public opinion are well known.

It does not seem that the theocratic Jewish state ever functioned well. The "judges" who succeeded Moses had spasmodic authority. Samuel founded the monarchy, which marks a divorce between Church and State. From then on, kings who are too human will rule Israel as earthly sovereigns. The official Church will support them. Divine authority will be embodied in the prophets, who will endeavor to lead Israel back toward theocracy. Such a return, they say, will permit the fulfillment of God's promises, according to which the Jews are to have dominion over all the world. In response to the prophets' appeals, partial returns take place, but they do not correspond to national successes. In the minds of certain prophets, the greatest, the vision of a chosen people takes the form of a spiritual Israel, suffering and dispersed throughout the earth, led by a Messiah of gentleness, the redeemer of all mankind. This vision was to become reality seven hundred years later with the coming of Jesus and the founding of the Church.

During the first three centuries of its existence, the Christian Church answered to the will of its founder. It was, in the heart of the Roman Empire, a chosen people, suffering and dispersed, living by grace alone, the prophet of a holy and merciful God. But a profound transformation took place under Constantine. The Roman state, as it began to totter, sought to steady itself on the sturdiest moral force in its midst, the Christian Church. It granted the Church authority and privileges. In exchange, the Church blessed the imperial banners. It was a return to the time of Moses, but the covenant was between the State and the priests. The prophetic Church had no place in it.

The collapse of the Roman Empire did not clear the atmosphere. The practice of infant baptism had generalized the idea that the Church was entered by a rite independent of the will, and not by personal conversion to Jesus Christ. For the disciples of the Church of Christ had been substituted the Christian State, or Christendom. Charlemagne, and then the Popes, tried to unify Christendom. Their efforts were in vain. Every national sovereign, assuming more or less arbitrarily the title "King by the Grace of God," was blessed by the papacy. The Reformation brought no fundamental change to the Catholic pattern. Luther limited the Church to the domain of the salvation of souls, according the princes the power of the sword "by divine right," and thus paving the way to a divorce between a Church specialized in its function as a comforter, and a state secularized but invested by God with the function of dispensing justice. In so doing, he opened the way to modern nationalism. Calvin went back to the Old Testament. He attempted at Geneva a return to the Mosaic theocracy. His disciples, the Puritans, were victims of a similar error in the states of New England. Fortunately (we say fortunately, what a paradox!) the multiplicity of the Protestant sects saved the Calvinist school from being obsessed with the idea of a Christianized state under the thumb of the Church.

Every one of these sects represents an attempted return to primitive Christianity. We deplore their spiritual pride and often their eccentricities. Their divisions are the scandal of Protestantism. But let us recognize that the prophetic character of the Church was revived through them, while in Catholicism it was perpetuated only in the lives of a few saints. Christian missions, which were the fruit of the religious revivals, so long as they remained supranational and nonviolent, gave the Church of the 19th century an heroic flavor of primitive Christianity.

But the Christendom of today accelerates its own decay. Its colonial imperialism and the two internal wars that have ravaged it leave the world nothing but the vision of a civilization which, under cover of a few great principles vaguely drawn from the Gospel (liberty, justice, truth) serves the barely disguised interests of certain nations and certain social classes. The Church, torn within by internal wars—at once victim of the situation and party to the acts committed—although it no longer blesses, as it did in 1914, the flags of the opposing camps, is yet allowing itself to slide into the position of promoting the strangely pessimistic doctrine that the Christian's duty is to defend his country, always the object of an unjust aggression. So, equally sincere believers continue to slaughter each other on the battlefields, convinced that they are acting in accordance with the purposes of God, who mysteriously includes holocausts among the methods he adopts for the accomplishment of his holy will.

It is time that the Church, returning to a study of its origins, recovered a sense of its mission within the State. It is commonly claimed that Jesus said nothing about the relationship between Church and State. Is this true? The

State in the time of Jesus was represented by two authorities: the Jewish authority, theocratic in type, consisting
of the Sanhedrin in Jerusalem; and the occupying authority, in the person of the Roman procurator. Jesus
addressed himself to each of these on several occasions.
He never associated himself with their activities, nor did
his disciples. Nor did Saint Peter, Saint Paul or Saint
John ever make the slightest allusion to any sort of col-
laboration between Church and State in the pursuit of
common ends. At most they advocate, and themselves
adopt, a nonviolent attitude toward the civil authority.
Their role as prophets impels them to utter warnings and
pronounce severe judgments against the State, but never
brings them to the point of armed revolt. Jesus dissociated
himself from the "maquis" of his time, the Zealots, who
wanted to free their country from the Roman yoke by
force of arms and to proclaim the temporal reign of God
on earth.

Jesus defines the place of the Church in the world in
terms of a function: the world is the soil, the Church the
agent by which the seed is sown. The world is a house,
the Church the candle placed on a candlestick. The
world is a field where the tares, which are the wicked, and
the wheat, which is the Church, grow side by side. The
Church is the mustard seed which becomes a great tree.
The world is the flour, the Church the leaven mixed in
by God to make the dough rise. The world is the sea containing fish of all kinds, the Church is the net cast into it
by the angels. The world is the earth, the Church its salt
and light. Thus, between the world and the Church there
is no discontinuity. The Church needs the world. Is it
possible to imagine a seed without soil in which it can

grow, a net without sea, leaven without dough? But the Church's function is always clearly defined. The Church is not the world; it has not to undertake the tasks of the world; it is not responsible for assuming direction of the world's affairs. The world cannot expect the Church to meet all its demands. The image that springs to mind is that of the world as a complete organism with all its nutritive, digestive and operative functions, but which would be no more than a body without purpose so long as its higher function, that of the spirit, failed to carry out the tasks intended for it. In itself the earth is barren, but the organic union with it of the seed creates a new dimension: life. The notion of the world as an organism is so clearly expressed in the Bible, from the Old Testament to the apostles, and passing through Jesus, that its validity as revealed teaching cannot be doubted. It corresponds, too, to all that Pascal felt, to everything that science confirms today in its discovery of similar structures, from the infinitely small to the infinitely great.

It does not seem that Jesus drew a clear-cut distinction between what he calls "the world" and the state. Is not the state merely one of the complex and very concrete forms in which the world, with its needs and functions, is concentrated in the form of larger or smaller cells: family, city, province, nation, confederation? The size of the state can vary. The family is already a state in embryo; European federation or the UN are perhaps states in the process of formation. The size makes little difference; the same tendencies will always be apparent. The state coordinates and polices human needs and activities; it represents a certain order, endeavoring to reconcile contradictory interests and suppress crime. All this takes

place in the realm of the relative. The state is secular, and
should remain so. That is, it should not claim to be absolute, even if its institutions are the fruit of the deposit left
by the religious traditions of the past. The state is not prophetic and should not tend towards theocracy. It stands
under the judgment of God, as all human activities. That
is all that can be said about it. God desires its conversion
as he desires the conversion of every individual, but since
the state is only the expression of the needs and activities
of individuals, there is no reason why the individual
should be more exacting toward the state than he is
toward himself. Why should the state be more righteous
than its citizens? How can the state be nonviolent, pacific,
disarmed, so long as the man who demands these things
of his government himself remains fearful for his interests,
egoistic and vindictive? Jesus has described the relationship between Church and State admirably in the parable
of the unrighteous judge.

Jesus tells us first of all about a town, which we must
picture as one of those of the New Testament: the towns
of Galilee or the Decapolis, little cities enjoying a certain
autonomy, meeting the whole range of their populations'
needs, and offering them all the usual features of organization. It is a miniature state, a cell within a great state.

At the head of the municipality is a magistrate, a
judge; the title itself shows that he is there, not as sovereign master, but to apply the law and to settle differences.
In chapter 12, verse 14 of the Gospel of Luke, Jesus refuses to assume the role of "judge" ("krites," arbitrator).
He will not divide the inheritance of the two brothers in
conflict. Thus the function of the magistrate is very

clearly defined: he is at the head of the social organism as arbitrator in the disputes that arise within it.

In the town described by Jesus, the judge has neither fear of God nor respect for man. The text says literally: "He would not turn back for man." How severely Jesus judges the authorities of his time. Pilate and Herod come to mind, and the great contempt of the Romans for colonial peoples denied the dignity of Roman citizenship. Is Jesus offering us a picture here of a God who paradoxically is "unjust" but will yield to prayer? In so far as his contemporaries, as some of our own, held God responsible for the injustices of the world, perhaps so. "You form your own pictures of the supreme judge according to your impressions of earthly life," Jesus would then say. But the precision of the description he gives of our magistrate leads us to suppose he is alluding to the actual situation in Palestinian towns under occupation: shady tax-gatherers, brutal Roman centurions, corrupt judges with no fear of God's law and despising the men they were supposed to govern in accordance with that law.

Are things much better in our own time? Certainly, parliamentary democracy has attempted to guarantee men the exercise of their fundamental rights, but the power of money still holds sway. The world is still divided between master-peoples, enjoying their full rights, and subject-peoples who are colonized and exploited. The whites don't notice it because they are on the right side of the fence. Then again, by a sort of tacit agreement between public opinion, the press and the state, the preponderating influence of financial interests is passed over in silence. The same thing holds true among nations, in peacetime, but most markedly in time of war. Then the judge reveals his true character; the question of governing in the fear of God does not even arise for him. In wartime the Ten Commandments, the Sermon on the Mount and the Great Commandments cannot be included among the stage-properties of the state. What would become of us if our government "turned back" for a man dying on a battlefield, for a woman or a child trapped in a blazing house? Where would the state end if we indulged in such sentimentalism? So Jesus seems to accept as inevitable the injustice of the town's administration. The rich and powerful triumph, the poor, the widows and the orphans are exploited. "What can I do about it?" cries the unjust judge. "It has always been like this; I rule in concrete situations and I can't escape into a utopian dream world. Human nature is bad and I have to reckon with it." Agreed, Jesus seems to answer, but don't ask me to be a judge of this kind. Let the church not involve itself in state administration or the arbitration of human conflicts.

All would go "well," then, in the town described by Jesus, that is to say, everything would go according to the "ways of this world," were it not for the obstacle the judge found in his path: the widow. Widows in the Bible are always exploited. The loss of a husband stripped them of all rights until the day they married again. The widow in this parable stands for the Church. Jesus leaves us in no doubt on this point: in verse 7 he identifies her with "the elect." What richness there is in the parable. In one word Jesus defines the nature of the Church for us and its place in society. The scriptural view of history cannot be understood without admitting the idea of election. God chose a people for himself from among the nations:

Israel. The new Israel, which is the Church, is also elected, but it has no racial or geographical boundaries. Jesus chose, one by one, the men who were to be his disciples (Luke 6:13). Let us notice, in passing, that the problem of predestination is clarified and simplified if it is realized that Jesus chose his disciples as missionaries. The ultimate purpose of election is not first and foremost the salvation of the individual elected, but rather the function he is thus called upon to fulfill in the world. So it is for Israel and for the Church: "I will give thee for a light to the Gentiles."

Our Church is our widow, placed in the town to carry out her mission. She is poor, without influence and without rights. She is the little flock already described by the prophets as "the poor" or "the remnant of Israel"; she is among "those of low degree" celebrated by Mary in her song. May the powerful Church which is ours today rediscover its true nature.

But the poor widow is not resigned to her lot. She is not, indeed, a revolutionary, a Zealot, waiting to overthrow the judge's authority. She respects his authority even in its injustices, and she applies to him to obtain justice; but she will not give in and does not seek alms.

The widow has a rich and powerful enemy in the town. He has, up to now, always won his cases, for his money corrupts the judge. This enemy is undoubtedly "the force of evil itself: Satan." The Church is in direct and permanent conflict with evil. The secular authority can come to terms with it. The Church cannot. It will not compromise. It is striking to find that in verse 7, as in verse 3, the word in the mouth of Jesus is "ekdikeo," "seek satisfaction for a wrong." It is a very characteristic legal term: the Church feels that right is wholly on its side against Satan. It is the victim. It represents the interests of God on earth. It should defend them valiantly and obtain redress, and that in a very concrete manner before the human authorities. The complacency of the state in the face of evil is explainable. That of the Church, chosen to be the champion of God, is inexcusable.

Let us go a step further: here is the widow in intimate contact with the unjust state. Is she going to convert the state, bring it to repentance, to confess its fault and fall at the feet of God? No. After a lengthy resistance the judge, thinking the case over, confirms to himself his own callousness: he does not fear God and will not turn back for any man. Yet he is going to make an exception for the widow. She pesters him, comes back again and again to drive him crazy. To get rid of her, he sees justice done. In the same way, the man at home and in bed yields to the insistence of the friend who asks him for three loaves of bread. Does the judge give in merely because he is weary? Does not the worst tyrant feel some mysterious respect for the man of courage?

The judge yields. He does not proclaim next morning that henceforth the Sermon on the Mount will be adopted as the state's constitution, but he has given in on one point, and other plaintiffs, and the widow herself returning to the attack, will be able to invoke the precedent to obtain justice once again. In this way the Church will fulfill its function in society. The Church does not itself govern, but it is the cornerstone of divine justice, and the state must either build on it or else stumble over it to its own condemnation.

Some readers will say that in my commentary I have stretched the true meaning of the parable, which was intended (verse 1 tells us) merely to show us that we must "always pray and never lose heart." Yes. But the prayer that Jesus taught us, "Hallowed be thy name, thy will be done on earth, as it is in heaven, thy kingdom come," is this then simply an affair between God and the individual soul? Is it only concerning their *individual* salvation that the elect cry day and night to God? Is it only for *their* forgiveness, for the assurance of *their* salvation?

In our parable Jesus speaks of the need for justice of a far broader kind. The world is there in his thought, with the horrible tragedies of its perdition, the state too with its contempt for God and man, and the force of evil with its power to corrupt, and the Church in its frailty and its poverty. Then Jesus says to the Church: Pray, pray the prayer I have taught you, that is, claim from God the restoration of justice on the earth, a resounding victory for the Church over evil. So we see the Church not merely as a little flock of souls saved from death, awaiting, amid the disasters of a world given over to Satan, the final Judgment, which will wipe out the earth and re-establish the Church in accordance with its rights. No, for Jesus it is the world—the state, the unjust judge —that is encircled. Its position is a precarious one between God who holds it in his hand and judges it from on high, and the Church which it persecutes but whose senseless prayer will be answered. For the judge will be obliged to yield, so persistent are the widow's pleas. Our prayer is a lever, its fulcrum God. Bearing down on it with all its weight in the name of divine justice, the

Church moves the mountain of injustice which is called the world: and will not God, said Jesus, see justice done to His elect, will he delay? I tell you, he will do them justice quickly.

This parable, rich in sensational developments, ends with a new twist. At the beginning Jesus seemed to be accepting the hypothesis current in the minds of the people that the world is unjust, and that God is a party to its injustice. In the second part of the parable, Jesus tells us: even if society is unjust and given over to Satan, you can, by praying and taking action, bring about changes in it, for your claims are in accord with God's will, and he is always ready to hear you. But in the third part Jesus says: it is God who seeks to introduce His justice on earth, it is He who makes the claims. However, He will do nothing without the Church. He expects the Church to have faith, that is, to intercede below as forerunner of the divine justice that comes from on high. If justice is not done promptly to the elect, if the widow continues to be exploited, if the judge persists in his contempt for God and man, if the Church remains unheard, the fault lies in its lack of faith, the spirit of its protests, its lack of a true spirit of prayer, and its tendency to compromise with evil and the unjust authorities of the world.

What a strange conclusion. The Church, unfaithful, is no longer to be compared to a widow suffering injustice, but to the salt of the earth that has lost its savor and is, therefore, responsible for the corruption of the world.

Jesus ends his parable with a question: What will happen if, on the day of his return, the Son of Man finds his Church unfaithful? He gives no answer. In Matthew

24:51 he tells the parable of the servant who, given authority over his master's household with the responsibility of issuing supplies at the appropriate times, starts to beat his fellows because his master is slow to return: "He shall cut him asunder," says Jesus, "and appoint him his portion with the hypocrites." This is a terrible judgment! May it not fall on our Church, on ourselves as Christians! It is no light responsibility being a member of a Church chosen to be the light of the nations.

But, objects the reader, the parable of the widow applies to a corrupt state. What is to be done when, as in the countries of the West, the state, without being Christian, has nevertheless been sufficiently influenced by the Church in the past to offer men a minimum of justice with the guarantee of their fundamental rights? Must this state be abandoned into the hands of non-believers? In refusing to defend it, do not Christians risk hastening its decline and so finding themselves a party to the ruin of the fragile edifice of freedom erected by the faithfulness of their fathers? If this were the case, they would have contributed to one of the tragic regressions of history. Let us state at once our view: it is our faithfulness today that will insure the survival of the democratic state, and lead to the conquest of a new freedom and a new justice. On the other hand, service given blindly to this same state through fear of dangers threatening it from within and from outside will be the real factor leading to its decay. The freedoms we have gained, regarded as privileges to be defended, become burdens for the peoples we exploit without realizing it. Regressions in history occur when regimes become fossilized through refusing to open themselves to higher forms of justice.

So the Church ought not to support the state blindly, even if the state protects it. In another parable, Jesus instructs us concerning the nature of the assistance the Church can give a state that is well-disposed towards it.

In Matthew's gospel the parables of the candle giving light to the house and of the eye as the light of the body are given separately. The first (5:15) describes the Church as the light of the world; it must make its good works shine before men. While the second (6:22), less precise, seems to apply solely to the lamp of the body in the individual, the eye of the conscience. But in Luke 11: 33 the two parables are welded together and their analogy is striking. The lamp in the house lights all those who come in. The eye, the lamp of the body, lights up the whole body; no part of it remains in darkness.

Jesus spoke so often of light and identified himself with it: "I am come as a light into the world" (John 8:12) and "I am the light of the world" (John 9:5); he was so plainly inspired by the prophecy of Isaiah, "I will also give thee for a light to the Gentiles" (49:6); he so explicitly marked out his disciples as the children of light, so clearly called them to be the light of the world, that it is impossible to regard this teaching as marginal, as no more than episodic in the thought of Jesus. So revelation confirms the validity of what we have called the organic function of the Church in the world. The parable of the eye as the light of the body defines quite naturally this function of the Church in the world, which it identifies with the function of the conscience in the body. The Church is the world's conscience.

Here then is a house where men come in and go out, and here a body with its different functions, digestive, motor and coordinating. All parts of the house, or of the body, answer to the requirements of a certain order. All are specialized, each in its own way. In the same way, society has organs, of which the state coordinates the activities. Among these organs there is one, the lamp or the eye, whose function is essential. It exists in its own right, being neither the table, nor the stool, nor the stove, nor the foot, nor the hand, nor the stomach. To express ourselves more biblically we will say: the eye, or the lamp, has been called by God, separated, prepared in advance, to contribute to the order of the body. It is a functional election, more clearly marked even than in the parable of the widow. But while the mission to which the widow is called is one of contradiction, the function of the lamp and the eye is constructive. They contribute to the organization of the house or the body without apparent friction or conflict. The eye can accept from the other members of the body the services it needs. It can be nourished with their blood, protected by their white corpuscles. There is no shame in that. Yet this dependence does not mean that the eye must feel itself so indebted to the other organs that its originality becomes an offense. It should not, through false humility, renounce the exercise of its particular function, which is to see. In giving up seeing, the eye would not only be untrue to the vocation assigned to it by Providence, but it would also betray the body itself which has need of its light. Jesus has no esteem for the scribes and the Pharisees, the "blind guides who lead the people astray. When the blind lead the blind both shall fall into the ditch." So, in our twin parables he defines the essential duty of the disciples called by God to be the light of the world: "Remain true to yourselves, be light, no one lights a candle to put it under a bushel"; "One is not salt to lose one's savor"; "One is not an eye to be in the dark."

Yet the Church is in danger of becoming dim. It has happened very often in its history that the Church allows its visual faculty to be impaired, allows itself to be put under a bushel. Then darkness falls upon the house and blind men run into and injure each other. The body plunged into darkness stumbles and falls. So with the state. Let the Church cease to exercise its illuminating function within it, and it goes under in obscurity and confusion.

The Church thinks it is expressing gratitude towards the state by making concessions to it. In reality, it is betraying it.

A scene at the Last Judgment, before the throne of God, might well be imagined. There, side by side in the dock, are the State and the Church. God, addressing first of all the State, asks for an account of its crimes: "Why did you tolerate the exploitation of the poor in your midst? Why have you oppressed, persecuted, tortured, murdered? Why did you make war on other nations, devastating their cities and killing men by the millions?" The State will bow its head; knowing it has sinned, it will ask for pardon, but it will also plead an extenuating circumstance: "The Church here," it will say, "was placed by you in my body to serve as an eye for me. An eye to contemplate you, O God of holiness, and to translate your commandments for me, expressing them in practical terms of my needs. It should have prophesied and shown me the way, at the risk perhaps of suffering at my hands. But it became rich; it became an institution; secular concerns tempered its zeal. It thought that concessions would lead me to understand it better, that I should be obliged to it for its indulgence towards my vices. Certainly I admit that, in my flesh, I preferred this Church which collaborated with me and gave me its blessing, but it was because of its blindness that I went astray. I accept your judgment, but ask that the Church be more severely condemned." Then God will turn to the Church and say: "Why did you say nothing when you saw the rich exploiting the people, why did you pretend not to know the facts when the State was oppressing, imprisoning, and torturing, why were you a party to its wars and why did you allow your members to take part in them? They went to neighboring countries to share in the massacre of thousands of men. It was not your part to be the infantryman's foot, the hand or the brain of the atomic technician, the arm of the artilleryman or the aviator, but the clear-sighted eye alert and ready to give the body of the State warning of the abysses toward which it was moving.

"You were my elect, but you have renounced your vocation. You thought you were of the world, and you were not; or rather, you were the little flock in the world and inseparable from it because you were charged with a special mission for it. Like Jonah, you have failed in your mission. Through your fault, the storm has broken loose and the ship almost foundered. If Jonah had not repented, Nineveh would have not heard his message. Nineveh would not have repented, and would have been destroyed. Now you have not followed Jonah on the path of repentance, and because of you I am obliged to condemn the state." Like the man of the parable, the Church will bow its head. It will be speechless. The divine judgment against it will be far more severe than against the State. The authorities of the State, as Saint Paul said of the Gentiles, "having no divine law are a law unto themselves," while the Church which "relies on the Law, priding itself on God, understanding his will, and with a sense of what is vital in religion . . . . persuaded that it is a guide to the blind, a light to darkened souls . . . . a teacher of other people who does not teach himself . . . ," the Church which prides itself on the Law dishonors God by its breaches of the Law. Because of it, the name of God is maligned among the Gentiles. We may be forgiven this borrowing of the apostrophe addressed by the apostle to the Jews. He would certainly say the same to the Church today, for grace has not been granted to the Church for its witness in the world to be weakened, but for its strength to be increased. The fact that the Church cannot bear witness to itself as the Pharisees did is no reason why its witness to the divine light should be diminished.

But let us come back to our parables. Against the eye that is evil, of bad quality ("poneros"), as the Greek text says, Jesus sets the eye that is single, generous, artless ("aplous"—directed toward one object). What is going to happen in the body? Well, exactly what happens in the house when a lamp is brought in and put on the table. The little oil lamps of Jesus' time were not very bright, but the difference between the total darkness of an unlighted house or a blind body, and the light shed by a lamp or an eye that is single, is the difference between zero and infinity. Henceforth, says Jesus, "*all* that are in the house have light . . . . They see your good works and they glorify your Father which is in heaven." "The body will be full of light, having *no* part dark, the whole shall be full of light, as when the bright shining of a candle doth give thee light." What good news for the Church! So often it is asked: "What use is your witness? Even your courageous preaching and your example of non-resistance and gentleness are ineffective. Your voice is lost in the night, no one hears it." So often the Church has doubts about itself. "The world," it tells itself, "must be able to grasp my message and my example; it is not capable of receiving the witness of a heavenly vision. Therefore, it is useless to demand saintliness and martyrdom of all Christians." Let the Church cease disturbing itself on this score then. If it remains silent, if it becomes dull, the world will be in darkness; but if it shines with divine light, if it gives quite simply an account of what it sees to the body, by its word and the example of its members, then the whole body will be illuminated. Enlightened by the Church, it will know better how to manage itself. Jesus adds this warning for the Church: "Take heed therefore that the light which is in thee be not darkness." Here we are back to our first parable. Politics are not the Church's business. That is to say, it is not for the Church to adopt such and such an attitude in order to obtain such and such a result. It has not even to practice pacifism, that is, reject arms with the object of stopping war. No, God expects one thing only of it: that it should walk in obedience to the Gospel, in total faith, refusing war because of that obedience, without concerning itself with the consequences, good or bad, that such refusal may involve. It is not the Church's business to establish peace between the nations. But it *is* its business to bear a witness to the love of God which cannot but imply refusal to kill. Such simplicity will light up the state and oblige it to put its house in order. We are not told that this order will bring universal peace. Peace belongs to God, and he has not promised us that. Jesus prophesies wars and rumors of wars. But what matter? Already in the past there have been astounding miracles of God's reaction to his people's suffering and faith. Let us take care then not to render such miracles impossible through our lack of faith.

Here is the place to refute energetically a theory, with little Gospel support, that has spread through the Church in recent years. Conscientious objection, it is said, is a special vocation. Certain believers are called to oppose evil in a more radical manner than the Church as a whole. They have assumed a prophetic ministry. The Church recognizes this ministry and prays for them. It even presses the state to recognize in law the citizen's right to conscientious objection in countries where such recognition is not yet given.

It is true that in his first epistle to the Corinthians Paul describes the diversity of ministries within the Church. He distinguishes the apostolic ministry, the prophetic ministry, the ministry of teaching, of working miracles, of healing, of "speaking with tongues," of interpreting. He does not speak here of a ministry common to the whole Church. Each one of us, says Saint Paul, receives "his manifestation of the Spirit for the common good." He describes the Church as a body in which different personal gifts play the parts of different limbs. He is speaking of the Church in its diversity. But there is no question of the existence in the Church of a specialized ministry of poverty, or goodness, or purity, or peacemaking, or conjugal fidelity, or truthfulness, non-resistance to evil, love for enemies, prayer, forgiveness of trespasses, trust in God, forbearance in judgment. All these things are recommended by Jesus and the apostles for the whole Church, that is, for all Christians. There is no dual morality in the Church, one code for saints, monks and priests, and another for ordinary believers. At most, we might conclude from certain words of Jesus that there is a vocation of celibacy. But can we speak of a vocation of purity? Clearly, purity is desired by God from everyone. Can we speak of a vocation of truthfulness? Clearly, all Christians are called upon to be truthful. In the same way, there cannot be a special vocation called "nonviolence." Violence, anger, murder are sins. No special vocation is needed to receive God's order not to sin. If it is a question of ministries, may we be shown to what sins the special vocations within the Church correspond? Where is the sin of not being an apostle, of not prophesying, of not being an expounder of the Scriptures, of not having the gift of miracles, of healing, of tongues? Saint Paul himself shows that all these magnificent gifts have been added to the common treasury for the glory of God in the Church. Yet, they are nothing without charity, which is the key to all. Charity is superior even to faith and hope. So no one comes to tell us it is necessary to have a special vocation to live in charity and so bear witness before men to the love of God. According to the sacerdotal prayer prayed by Jesus, the entire Church is called to bear witness to the unity of God and to the union between God and Jesus, which is divine love, and the unity of the disciples among themselves, which is Christian love made possible by the presence of Jesus in them. Without this unity, this charity, the world cannot believe in one God and in the unique ministry of love accomplished by Jesus in the world.

So, without even mentioning love toward non-Christians, which is required no less in witness to the divine sacrifice, the entire Church cannot but abide in a mutual love that excludes anger, hate and murder, and hence participation in wars that lead Christians to kill one another. The order "love one another" is irreconcilable with "kill one another." It cannot be a question here of a particular vocation. It is a question of the whole Church continuing the ministry of Jesus on earth. If the Church is not faithful to that ministry, each of its members is responsible for its failure. It is for each one to ask himself: "What am I doing to express, at the same time as the ministry of purity, truthfulness, honesty, gentleness, the Church's ministry of charity? If I am unfaithful to it, it is because I lack faith. I lack the courage to follow my master so far, but it is not because I have not the vocation of charity!" Come, let us be honest with ourselves, and sincere repentance and God's forgiveness will put us on our feet again for renewed obedience.

Chapter 9

God's Time and Man's

OUR LIFE IS STEEPED IN A MYSTERY THAT IS CALLED time. Einstein, the mathematician, describes it as the fourth dimension, as a result of which space can expand to infinity or contract to zero. Our intelligence is incapable of grasping what it cannot experience. The fact is, we live in time, and we believe that God dominates time: "a thousand years in thy sight are but as a single day." How are we to make this faith a part of our lives? This is the problem that each of us has to solve at every moment of his existence.

Time is perceptible to us in two forms: the horizontal, linear form, which we will call man's time, and a vertical form which we will call God's time. Horizontal time unwinds like a ribbon set in motion at the creation, and which will stop, we suppose, at "the end of time." The part of the ribbon already unwound is the past, the past of mankind, which is history, and our own past as individuals, from the day of our conception to the present moment. The past constitutes an experience; without it

I should not exist. The past lends itself to analysis. By studying it I can, in so far as I remember the various causes that fashioned it, determine the effects of such causes. Analysis offers me a picture of a universe that is, as it were, closed, complete, where all events take place necessarily. The past can yield me no knowledge of freedom. It is as a result of studying the past that modern science has arrived at the idea of determinism. Today it is discovering, on the borders of exact knowledge, that there is a possibility of freedom, but for the purposes of practical living, this has no more interest for us than Einstein's fourth dimension.

The part of the ribbon not yet unwound forms the future. Men are more concerned about the future than they are about the past. They spend most of their time and energy conjecturing what the future will bring and regulating their conduct accordingly. The peasant foresees the return of spring; he sows. The mother foresees the cold weather; she knits woolens. The workman foresees the increase of his family; he seeks to improve his wages. The student foresees the examination that will admit him to the university; he works. The prudent man foresees the visit of the thief; he puts bolts on his doors. The manufacturer foresees the wear and tear of his machines, increased competition from his rivals, and the recurrence of an economic crisis; he capitalizes. A state foresees the possibility of aggression by an enemy nation, and it arms. Jesus repeatedly recommended his disciples to have forethought. There is nothing wrong in being prepared. It is one of the virtues proper to man and at the root of all civilization.

How can a man foresee the future? By analyzing the

past. The past has shown him that the same causes pro-
duce the same effects. He can test the truth of this law by
experiment. His analysis of the recent past reveals to him
the causes which are determining the course of events in
the world. It is, therefore, not difficult for him to look into
the future. In the name of the experience of the past
which he projects into the future, he builds a scheme in
which all contingencies are provided for. If he remains
vaguely conscious of an element of chance he cannot master, it is because he cannot calculate in advance all the
causes that will be operative tomorrow or in a year's time.
His sense of being a gambler amidst the hazards of life is
counteracted by his awareness of a destiny he cannot alter
bearing him along toward an end fixed in advance by the
blind force which is nothing more than the "meeting" of
all the causes and their determined effects.

Our life, alas, is spent in the past—in memories and
often in regrets—and in the future—in preparation and
often in fear. Once the car is in gear after the carefree
years of childhood, the man is carried along helplessly.
The vague dream of happiness and freedom he cherished
in his youth is replaced by the burden of a yoke on his
shoulders which he must bear for his conscience' sake
without being too sure why, until the day he dies as an individual, while history rolls ceaselessly on toward its dis-
tant end.

These descriptions, however, omit one element: the
consciousness of existence, the feeling that permits us to
say "I." Now in the moment when I write this line, when
I form this thought, when I pronounce this word "I," I
am there between the past and the future, filled with a
wonderful awareness of my presence to myself. Let us

continue our comparison: if I take a pair of scissors and cut the ribbon of time as it unwinds, the cut is called "now" and the two parts "yesterday" and "tomorrow." In fact I never live "yesterday" any more than I live "tomorrow." It is *now* that I exist, that I think, speak, act, eat, work. I know very well that this "now" has no thickness, no more than a geometrical line. Yet it is as real as the line that separates an object from the surrounding air, and since it exists, it is worth while concentrating my attention upon it. It is even obvious that the more a man can concentrate on the "now" the more alive he is, for it is now that the brain thinks; it is in the "now" alone of this concentrating brain that past and future, experience and conjecture, exist. Unfortunately very few people know how to live *now*. Regret and anxiety beset their thoughts. They prefer these "distractions" to the dread they feel before the "now." It is true that it is rather frightening. Here I am, wholly responsible, faced with the evidence of my liberty. In this present moment there is nothing to prevent me from jumping out of the window, killing my neighbor or giving him all my goods. This freedom is a terrible void which makes me take flight toward the more reassuring zones of a determined past and a determined future. Indeed, the existentialist position is tragic if man considers himself forsaken. And atheistic existentialists do hasten to fill the "now" with desires of the flesh. In so doing they abandon, without admitting it to themselves, the existentialist position, to revert to the slavery of dreams and the senses, which in their turn are governed by our determined past.

To maintain the existentialist attitude, it is necessary to practice what mystics call silence. It is not a matter of desiring an external object, or of desiring oneself as one is or other than one is; it is a matter of entering into oneself in the present moment. Now it is there, within, after the "noises" of the earth have been eliminated, that God is to be found. "When you pray," said Jesus, "go into your room and shut the door, and pray to your Father *who is there* in secret." God is not the void; he is absolute; he is existence; he is the eternal present; he is the Presence that we are always fleeing because it is too pure. Now this God is a Father, that is to say, a voluntarily sacrificed purity, from whom pours down unceasingly a generous torrent which is paternal love.

But life, you will say, is going to reclaim its rights. I must make plans, take action, anticipate. I can't stay here doing nothing. How true this is! How pointless God's time would be without man's time, how futile the Spirit without incarnation. It would be motionless, the philosophers tell us, and total immobility is already nonexistence. Thus Jesus, after his hours of ecstasy (and of temptation; the one borders on the other, for in the present moment lies freedom), came down to the plain and mingled with the suffering crowds to heal them. Only— and here is the vital point—God entered in that moment as a new cause to change the "chemical combination" of the past. A man who emerges from prayer (if he has really prayed, which is rare) is his past "plus" God, that is, his past turned, like a photographic print, from negative to positive by forgiveness. Saint Paul says (2 Cor. 5: 7): "He is a new creature: old things are passed away; behold all things are become new." This newness profoundly modifies the plans of this man: his future has become the future "plus" God. It is conceived in the freedom of the love of God. When we say "conceived," we use the word in its proper sense. Union does actually take place, between a loving God and determined reality, through the channel of the man who prays. The fruit of this union will be a new unexpected being, reacting on circumstances renewed, transformed by its presence.

There are no clear-cut boundaries between prayer, ecstasy, and society, between God's time and man's. It is so obvious that the one cannot do without the other, that man's time, if it existed alone, would not be sufficient to explain itself. It cannot explain how the first being that said "I" appeared, nor how each forward step is taken in the evolution of such beings. Each step was in fact a marriage between an enslaved past and a "now" of God; and so the future was different. But just as, before each step, the beings, confined within their own laws, could not even imagine a new order of greatness, so long as it was not an accomplished fact, so today the world is incapable of imagining an order of greatness in which divine love will be supreme. But the man who has met God brings his own newness to the world and so helps it to take a step in faith into what, until now, was impossible. Tomorrow will bring disillusionment. Experience will come along to take the place of grace, but, said Jesus, the day's own trouble is sufficient for the day. He recommends us to have foresight, but not foresight without God. To anticipate our own incompetence is not looking forward, it is looking back. Indeed, there is no reason why the great silence that reigns in me now before God should not return again tomorrow. It even becomes increasingly probable that it will do so, for as the metal which, after having an electrical discharge passed through it, is a better con-

ductor, so the soul that has known contemplation is more
likely to relive the experience.

So a man's history will be written like a mountain
range against the sky, in terms of its summits. It is the
summits that are measured. The foot of the mountain has
no interest for the surveyor; it is there only to support the
crests. Why, then, am I obsessed by the fear of obstacles
and abysses? The counsel is not new which urged man to
fix his eyes on God. That is what is meant by "the gaze of
faith" (le regard de la foi).

And now what shall we say about the Church? It is very
simple. The Church is the link of prayer. Its sacraments
represent the vertical descent of God's time into the
matter of our bodies, the fabric of history. It is not always
easy to ask of the isolated individual that he assert himself
as the agent of the revolutionary power of the infinite,
against a world unwilling to believe in the possibility of its
own transformation. But God has given us the Church,
the society of those bound together, not by their own will
but by the divine will. He has called them by name with a
view to entrusting them with a mission to be undertaken
together. And it is for this Church—which exists only
from moment to moment in prayer, repentance, faith,
and in God's time, and which comes down every morning
from his mountain to heal—to plan a world which shall
be the past "plus" God. With what divine joy we shall be
filled on the day when the Church says once more to its
faithful: "There is God, there is Jesus, there is the Holy
Spirit; here am I, I the Church, and here are the orders
I give you on behalf of the Lord!" Then the walls of the
pagan city, of the unjust State, of the impregnable Jericho
will fall. And if there are no walls, if the human city

where we live is well-disposed, if the State is inclined to listen to the Church's proposals, well, what are we waiting for? All we have said will be only the more true. Let us, then, not make this a pretext for returning to the principles of the flesh.

Conclusion

Back to Man Again

THE MOMENT A GROUP OF MEN BELIEVES IT HAS A theory that is true, it is carried away by an urge it cannot resist to defend that theory with all the human weapons of controversy, censorship, persecution and war. The Church has not escaped this law, ever since it became estranged from its origin, which is conversion, a return to God—a God who is pleased "now" to tear down these barriers and allow his enemies to enter his territory and plunder the holiness and truth of his own property, which is his beloved Son. And more, these conquering foes have found no obstacles in their way. They have encountered only forgiveness; and it is they now who stumble over this forgiveness, stumble until they believe in it. For the time being, until the Last Judgment, the throne of vengeance is unoccupied. In the place of the avenging God there is what the Scriptures call "the lamb of God" which takes away the sin of the world. You hear, *"of the world."* Thus, while for us God remains the object of our adoration, the Alpha and the

Omega, the aim and end of all existence, it appears that for God the end is man. This good news is the essence of the Gospel message, the revolution which for theories has substituted a loving Person, and founded Christian humanism. God said: "Let us make man in our own image"; "The Son of Man is come to seek and to save that which is lost"; "It is not the will of your Father which is in heaven that one of these little ones should perish." How remote we are here from any theory! And how, if he is uncertain of the way he has to follow, is the Christian going to orient himself? We have seen that theories lead us astray. We have seen, too, that every one of us is incapable of doing good, that it is dangerous to believe our hands are clean, dangerous to reconstruct our own past for the sake of our cause, justifying ourselves artificially. Pharisaism is the worst of the risks run by Christians; it attempts to put us in the place of God. A moralizing religion, a religion of works, even of nonviolence, only raises the screen of pride between man and God, and the scandal of jealousy between men of virtue and evil-livers. What remains, then, to guide our conduct with a minimum of error? *A loving respect for our neighbor.*

Jesus sums up in two sentences the law and the prophets, that is, the duty of holiness and the prophetic mission of the Church in the world: "Thou shalt love the Lord thy God with all thy heart, and with all thy soul, and with all thy mind; and thy neighbor as thyself." The two commandments are found in the Old Testament. What is original in Jesus' teaching is that he brings them together and links them with a bond of identity. Our translators say that the second commandment is "like unto" the first.

The interpretation is weak. "Homoios" means equal, equivalent, the same. Jesus maintains, and the apostles after him, that we cannot love God if we do not love our brother, that we cannot be forgiven by God if we do not forgive our brother. We shall be judged according to our own judgment. This is the only point on which the teaching of Jesus is rigid. Why? Because the man who sets limits to his love toward his neighbor raises a wall between himself and the God who has abolished his own frontiers. Jesus is extraordinarily indulgent toward all sinners, he displays unbounded loving-kindness toward them, he never ceases to believe in the possibility of their turning from their wickedness; but he is uncompromising with hypocrites, that is, with the spiritually proud who have no love for their brothers and thus separate themselves from God. And so, having abolished the Mosaic law and its complicated requirements, he gives us a new commandment which is nothing but the translation into everyday language, through our bodies, of the person and the work of God: Love your neighbor, serve him, heal him, even if this means the violation of other traditional or formal laws, give in to him rather than offend him and turn him away from God. Don't make yourself an obstacle on his way to God. It is a matter of a direct return, elementary to man, a question of human realism, disarmingly simple, in which the neighbor's physical life is as important as his spiritual life, where the healing of the body and the healing of the soul are joined in a single operation. Because of the God-present-to-myself, I am intensely real, existing, present to myself "now," and my neighbor enjoys the same privilege of existence. I am liberated from fears, from plans, from complicated orders issued by the state in peacetime as in wartime. Freed from all casuistry, I shall share with joy all service to man, but refuse with the same joy all attempts on man's existence. I shall no longer allow myself to be impressed with the great principles quoted to me, with historical situations, with call to sacrifice my blood. Every enterprise undertaken in the service of man, for the benefit of children, of the persecuted, of prisoners, of the exploited, of the aged and the infirm, will have my approval and support. The Christian objector to military service is not a purist who, on the day he receives the order to kill his neighbor, wakes from his dream to say "no." He is a servant with experienced hands who is so busy helping his neighbor that to interrupt his activity to undertake the task of a murder is unthinkable to him.

Certain disturbing problems remain: what is to be done to rescue the innocent from the clutches of their persecutors, to prevent criminal regimes from destroying life, to check evildoers, to save the victims of exploitation and torture? No theoretical answer can be given to these questions. Events create circumstances which are never exactly the same. For those who yesterday conscientiously believed it their duty, for love of their neighbor, to take part in an act of violence, a movement of armed resistance or a war of liberation, the problem is still there. They should not say: My experience of the past proves to me that the future will be like this or like that. If violent remedies employed against tyrants have put an end to certain forms of evil, they have not eliminated Evil. Evil itself has taken root again elsewhere. The fertilizer that stimulates its growth is yesterday's violence, even if it appeared "justified." We have seen that the future of a man who prays "now" is not determined by his past. He is free of the acts he committed yesterday. But his past, forgiven by God, creates the possibility of an entirely new future. So he can make plans for saving his neighbor and courageously reject anything that leads to or brings about his destruction.

And yesterday's conscientious objector is not satisfied either. He is troubled because he has not been able to make a visible contribution to the checking of evil, and because indirectly his own hands are stained with his brothers' blood. Will he resign himself next time to taking up arms? By no means. His past, plus God, will open doors to him that now seem shut. The cycle of violence is closed upon itself. Even "justified" murder brings vengeance in its train, "legitimate" defense, and always fresh crimes. The sacrifice of Jesus, however, has opened an unexpected way to possibilities that are constantly renewed. This is the way the Church should boldly follow. The State can only work from the past to anticipate the future and determine its policies. As long as it is abandoned by the Church, it knows nothing of repentance. But the Church in its midst does know repentance, and it knows *only* that, and it bears witness of that before the State, for the healing of the State.

If the Church does not surpass the State in justice, it does not belong to the kingdom of God; it leaves the lost to themselves in the agony of their abandonment.

Meanwhile Jesus, even if deserted by his Church, climbs the road to Calvary, continuing alone to seek and to save those that are lost.